Market Insanity

Perspectives in Behavioral Economics and the Economics of Behavior

Market Insanity

A Brief Guide to Diagnosing the Madness in the Stock Market

Michael Taillard

Series Editor
Morris Altman

ACADEMIC PRESS

An imprint of Elsevier

Academic Press is an imprint of Elsevier
125 London Wall, London EC2Y 5AS, United Kingdom
525 B Street, Suite 1800, San Diego, CA 92101-4495, United States
50 Hampshire Street, 5th Floor, Cambridge, MA 02139, United States
The Boulevard, Langford Lane, Kidlington, Oxford OX5 1GB, United Kingdom

Notices

Knowledge and best practice in this field are constantly changing. As new research and experience
broaden our understanding, changes in research methods, professional practices, or medical treatment
may become necessary.

Practitioners and researchers must always rely on their own experience and knowledge in evaluating and
using any information, methods, compounds, or experiments described herein. In using such information
or methods they should be mindful of their own safety and the safety of others, including parties for
whom they have a professional responsibility.

To the fullest extent of the law, neither the Publisher nor the authors, contributors, or editors, assume any
liability for any injury and/or damage to persons or property as a matter of products liability, negligence
or otherwise, or from any use or operation of any methods, products, instructions, or ideas contained in
the material herein.

Library of Congress Cataloging-in-Publication Data
A catalog record for this book is available from the Library of Congress

British Library Cataloguing-in-Publication Data
A catalogue record for this book is available from the British Library

ISBN: 978-0-12-813115-2

For information on all Academic Press publications
visit our website at https://www.elsevier.com/books-and-journals

  Working together
to grow libraries in
developing countries

www.elsevier.com • www.bookaid.org

Publisher: Candice Janco
Acquisition Editor: Graham Nisbet
Editorial Project Manager: Susan Ikeda
Production Project Manager: Joy Christel Neumarin Honest Thangiah
Designer: Mark Rogers

Typeset by VTeX

Dedication

An Open Letter to Accounting and Financial Professionals: Your field provides a more reliable and detailed record of human history than any other. It is a profession of creating and using records that, by necessity, must be free of embellishment or interpretation in order to be functional. There is no revisionism declared by a class of ruling or conquering leaders. There is no morality-based controversy by which people of a faith might feel the need to alter a reality, no matter how obscure or private. There is only the need for accuracy in recording and maintaining information about resources and the transactions of those resources which occur. It is a quantitative field of measurement, devised from its inception to prevent misinterpretation or the intervention by shysters.

The invention of the written language did more to shape human development and the ability of societies to function than just about anything you can think of, and was critical to the development of fundamental mathematics. Without the invention of the written language, modern society would fail to develop even in its most fundamental forms, and this invention owes its existence entirely to the fields of accounting and finance. The first language, known as Cuneiform, was developed for the purpose of recording business transactions, using small clay tablets as receipts, inventory records, and other matters of daily financial operations. These were so important, that they also inspired the first envelopes, in which these clay receipts were placed inside thin hollow clay shells that were only broken upon completion of the transaction, so that there was no question about counterfeiting the contents of the records.

Consider how much data you handle and store at any given time for your company or clients. How long do you maintain those archives before they are purged? Maybe you keep records for 15 years? At most, you might keep them for 20 years? It is almost certain, as it is among the majority of people, that the oldest records in your archives are less than 10 years old. Now consider the age of your company – the year it was formed. Now each of these ancient remnants is considered priceless as a source of knowledge about our own origins and history – a true history of humanity, which tells a real story that transcends the machinations of those who try to define history, yet around the world, exhibits of ancient currency and trade such as at the Detroit Institute of the Arts are left abandoned, with the last expert on their exhibit retiring many years ago without a replacement.

Coming back to the modern day, how old is the company for which you work? How much history has been lost while purging the archives of old financial records? What value would these records have had as data to modern researchers working to understand the mechanics of the world around us and improve upon the methods currently being used? What value would these records have had to future generations as they strive to better understand the people and events that led to the nature of their current civilizations?

The records you purge are of great value today, and will be priceless in the future. Though you likely sort through countless volumes of data on a regular basis, most of it mundane or even useless to you in your current endeavors, remember that it is an invaluable source of understanding for others. Each record you destroy is a small piece of human history that is now forever lost.

It is with this understanding that I implore you to reconsider your current protocol for destroying old records.

Simply put: Stop it.

Michael Taillard

Contents

About the Author

Michael Taillard, PhD MBA

Michael Taillard is a private economic consultant, emphasizing applied strategy and quantitative behavioral research. His other works include titles like Corporate Finance for Dummies (John Wiley & Sons), and Aspirational Revolution: The Purpose-Driven Economy (Palgrave Macmillan). He has taught and created original course content for universities around the world.

Preface

This book, oh my dear reader, is not one that contains any information that is entirely new nor entirely profound when taken individually. Having decided to read this book, it is likely that you will be familiar with at least some of the basics contained within, since it is within the nature of the topic of this book that by having decided to read it you most likely already have some interest either in economics or psychology. Rather, this is a topic currently considered to be interdisciplinary – combining elements of both into a very new area of research called behavioral economics. It is the nature of this book, then, that it utilizes the works of many modern researchers in this new branch of behavioral science to finally make some sense of what is happening in the stock market. This falls into a specific sub-discipline called behavioral finance, if you really enjoy labeling things (and who does not enjoy labeling everything into narrow categories!). The end result is a book which contains a few things you know and a few things you do not to explain a lot of recent discoveries related to human behavior in matters of money.

The way this book is written is to provide some of the basics from both psychology and economics for the sake of people who have studied only one or neither, and then applying them in new ways (but only as appropriate given the existing research) to the benefit of everyone. From the perspective of an economist, this means addressing how the mind works and the manner in which the mechanics of the brain inherently shape investing decisions, shaping the whole of global capital markets. From the perspective of a psychologist, this means looking into how the unique environments and novel measurements afforded by economic research provides insight into the mechanics of human brain and the broader implications these have for understanding the behaviors of individuals and groups.

I hope you enjoy reading this book. Maybe you learn something new, and that will be great, too, but enjoyable books sell better, so let us focus on that. Cheers!

Chapter 1

Introduction

The only investing advice I ever give anyone is to never trust anyone giving you investing advice. If you came to this book wanting to know whether you should invest in some call options of Class-A convertible shares for a dog grooming start-up from Namibia cross-listing on the US OTC market, then you should absolutely read this book because you will learn to avoid making that sort-of mistake again in the future. No, you will not learn to avoid the mistake of making bad investments because, as I said, this is not that type of book. Anyone who promises you they can guarantee you will not make a bad investment is full of crap. Even assuming they are competent (which is a rarity, in itself), there is no guarantee they are not corrupt. Instead, by reading this book you will learn to avoid mistakes like taking investing advice from books that promise to make you rich on the stock market. Quite frankly, that is what this books is really about – the dumb decisions we make, why we make them, and the impact they have on our investments. None of the things we do are as prudent or sensible as you think, and while reading this book it should become clear that I am taking full advantage of that – something which is a rare treat for both readers are writers, as far as academic books go.

The publisher has encouraged me to be "irreverent", allowing us to have a bit of fun with the contents of this book. Quite frankly, that was the point anyway, since we are basically talking about people acting like clowns, and the stock market has no shortage of clowns. The tone of the book is just a personal expression of the problems faced in the financial industry, though. That does not mean this book is cuts corners on the facts, though. Everything described in this book is based on valid, scientific research published in reputable journals, and there will be citations and references abound.

The research being compiled and described here, all on the topic of behavioral economics as applied to the stock market, is a sharp departure from traditional finance and economics books, which make assumptions like people acting rationally and the markets being efficient. There are some old-timers and undergrads out there who still hold onto those ideas, but they have been thoroughly debunked since the 1970s, when behavioral economics really developed as a field of study. In fact, among the various citations included in this book, you will notice a few names are mentioned multiple times, throughout. These are the pioneers of the field (aka: old), including:

Daniel Kahneman and Amos Tversky: Both quantitative psychologists by origin, they both delved into research on how people make decisions. Each of

Market Insanity. DOI: 10.1016/B978-0-12-813115-2.00001-X

them have their own unique careers and contributions, but their work together is considered by most to be the seminal point at which the field of behavioral economics was born. Together, they contributed a vast array of research and theory which solved problems that daunted economists using the assumption of rational decisions. The foundations of behavioral economics, including concepts such as psychological framing, and prospect theory, upon which much of the bulk of behavioral economics extends.

Robert Shiller: Shiller is an extremely influential economist, and the name-sake of the Case-Shiller Price Index, which is the predominant measure of real estate prices. Shiller dedicated most of his career to exploring the cause and nature of economic bubbles, particularly in real estate and other investment markets. It is because of Shiller that we now know the cause of bubbles is not a rational one, but rather they are the result of behavioral insanity.

George Akerlof: A prominent economics professor, he produced ground-breaking works into the economics of asymmetric information and the manner in which behaviors are exhibited under conditions of asymmetry. He also produced research on the economic impact of social identity, and choices made as a result of one's own perception of social status and the expectations laid upon them by the norms of that status.

The role of this book is not to make any major contributions to the field, although I do point-out a few things here and there, particularly in Chapter 7. The role of this book is to bring together all the research on behavioral economics available, both old and new, and summarize how it applies specifically to the actions of stock investors, translated into normal-people talk. Researchers, and economists especially it seems, like to use ridiculously complicated jargon; and it is in the nature of doing proper scientific research that studies must be written in a manner that is painfully tedious to read. Be honest, you and I both know that you have opted to skip the majority of more than 1 research paper, instead reading just the abstracts and conclusions. Well, rejoice and give thanks, because it is the entire point of this book to force me to read all the stuff you do not want to and then write about the interesting parts. While this does not sound like much, it does play an extremely important role because behavioral economics is a very new field of research, and since it combines elements of psychology and economics, it tends to be difficult for people to understand. Much of the criticism about behavioral economics comes from a lack of understanding about what is being accomplished. Sure, there are other books which do the same thing, but none of them focus on the implications of the field exclusively on the stock market, and apparently only the stock market warrants the author of an academic book to be snarky. Do not discount the importance of sarcasm and cynicism in books like this, either. It is important to be able to communicate with people in a way they will appreciate in order to hold their attention long enough to teach them something. So, if you were expecting something written in the formal snootiness of traditional academia, then you can give a sigh of relief now. At this point there seems to be a broad consensus that we need to improve our communication skills because historically our writings have been boring and hard for the general public to understand.

Before we jump into it, though, there is some basic concepts you need to know. I do not want you writing back to me ranting about how none of this is real science, or sending some long-ass manifesto on why you think all economists are wrong, because printer paper is expensive and I can light my firepit with much cheaper quality paper, improving our cooperative resource efficiency.

Let us start by establishing what economics and psychology really are. They are both forms of applied neurology. Economists use the scientific method to study peoples' behavior in terms of resource utilization and distribution, while psychologists use the scientific method to study peoples' behavior in terms of understanding their health and development. Both of these things stem from neurological processes in the brain, which means when you stick someone under a brain scanner (ideally and fMRI, but those things are really expensive to operate), you can actually see that wrinkled blob of an organ in your head go to work. Neurologists can study your brain and its functions, but would have no idea exactly how those functions cause you to act in different ways, just as economists and psychologists can explain how you will behave but rely on neurologists to explain what makes us behave the ways we do. Behavioral economists take all 3 of these things and smush them together to answers a question as old as humanity, itself: What the hell is wrong with us?

As far as the stock market goes, it is very much the epitome of the irrational human. The global stock markets are forums for people from all nations and walks of life to come together peacefully with the single goal of acting like utter fools (if ever there was proof that all people were created equal, it is our capacity to make fools of ourselves). In case you were not aware, the basic premise is this: Corporations are companies owned by stockholders. Ownership of the company is split into millions of pieces, and those pieces are sold to stockholders, so that they are paying to own a small part of the company. The stock market is the place where people go to buy and sell shares of ownership. Ideally, the point is to buy ownership in companies that are successful, so that the company will be worth more, resulting in the value of their ownership in that company being worth more. Then you can sell the stock to someone else at a higher price than you bought it. Simple enough? Good, because we are going to spend the rest of the book explaining why people take this seemingly simple idea and turn it into one of the most complicated things you can imagine.

When I say "people", what I really mean is investors. There are lots of different types of investors, including people who just stick money in their retirement accounts and hope for the best. Some chapters of this book apply to the hands-off investors who would rather have a real life they can enjoy, but for the most part we are talking about people who do this sort of thing for a living – either they are professional investors in some capacity, or they are amateurs who manage their own investment portfolios full-time from home. Either way, these active investors can be split into two broad categories: traders and value investors.

Value investors are people who look long and hard for companies that they think have a fantastic future ahead of them, and then buy those stocks while they are still nice and cheap. Value investors hold-on to their investments for the long-haul, ignoring the daily turbulence of the markets. Traders do not care so much about the individual companies as they do movements in the market. They try to take advantage of all the ups and downs, buying while prices are down and then selling them while they are high, doing this in high volume and making a little bit of money each time (if they are successful in doing it, which generally is not the case).

One final term you need to know is "portfolio". Anytime someone buys an investment, it is considered part of their portfolio. The reason we give it a special name is that once a person invests in a variety of different investments, then they can start performing analyses and managing strategies that take into consideration the way the different stocks interact together. For example, it is common for investors to hold some stocks that are very low risk, some that are moderate risk, and some that are extremely risky. They believe that there may be opportunity for massive gains in the extremely risky stocks, so they pursue them to a limited degree, ensuring the majority of their investment portfolio is dedicated to low or moderate risk stocks. Once you delve a bit deeper into the behaviors of investors, you will find that there are many different styles and strategies, but this is just Chapter 1. Let us take it slow and enjoy our time together.

For now, it is time for the obligatory summary of contents necessary for all non-fiction authors to include as a part of the introduction in order to avoid getting scolded by their publishers (help me!). The book is divided into chapters, and each chapter is divided into sections. The individual sections each talk about a specific type of behavioral anomaly, describing what it is, when and how it was discovered, how it makes you suck at investing, and what you can do to minimize or prevent it from occurring. Each of these sections are then clustered into chapters, based on common traits between them. There is a chapter dedicated to different type of biases (Chapter 3), for example, and another dedicated to flaws in perception of the world around us (Chapter 5), and another chapter dedicated to simply acting like a dummy (Chapter 4). To quote William Shakespeare, "Love is merely a madness; and, I tell you, deserves as well a dark house and a whip as madmen do; and the reason why they are not so punished and cured is that the lunacy is so ordinary that the whippers are in love too." So, certainly a chapter on the lunacy to which we are driven by our emotions is included (Chapter 6), and we take things a bit further in Chapter 7 to explore how prevalent mental illness truly is among investors and the manner in which specific ailments of the mind will influence our investing decisions. This particular organization not only makes the book easier to read because it is broken-up into smaller units so you do not have to worry about stopping mid-chapter, but this particularly style of organization also makes this book easier to use as a reference guide, should you find yourself in need of such a thing. Clearly Chapter 1 is merely an introduction, while Chapter 2 sets some foundations about the ridiculous notions of rationality and efficiency which so many economists and investors have assumed to be true for far too long; none of these 2 chapters hold to the same structure as the bulk of the book. There are also a conclusion and an afterword. The former is just a conclusion, and the latter touches on how we are driving to madness the very technologies that were developed to help prevent our own irrational decisions.

So, that about sums it up. Turn the page so you read something more interesting than an introduction chapter.

Chapter 2

The Rational Fallacy

We all like to think we are rational – that the decisions we make are based on informed assessments. Regardless of how little faith we have that those around us are capable of doing the same, we each convince ourselves that we alone can at least recognize what is best, even if we do not always opt to pursue it. Much of the society we have constructed is based on the assumption that, when taken collectively, the whole of our actions will be logical; but it takes some Olympics-level mental gymnastics to look at the stock market and deny the chaos. Fortunately for us, some of humanity's greatest minds have spent more than a century developing ways for us to cling to the belief that there is some grand pattern of efficiency built into the markets that is simply too complex for individuals to predict. There is even a treasure trove of mathematical equations which model the value or price of individual investments, or the markets as a whole, based on the idea that investors are able to optimize the value of their decisions. Thank goodness we can rest our minds easy and continue to pretend that markets are efficient and people are rational (or, at least, you are rational while everyone around you is an idiot). It is a comforting idea, really, to think that your retirement savings are safely in the hands of people who know what they are doing, or at least safely in the invisible hands of a market that automatically works-out for the best. It is also really easy to believe: Finance is nothing but numbers, right? There is no possible way people could be looking at the exact same numbers and come to different conclusions! No sir!

Well, I have got some bad news and some good news. The bad news is that we are all nuts. "I'm mad, you're mad. You must be or you wouldn't have come here." (Quote: Lewis Carroll) On a daily basis, the decisions we make deviate so far from rationality that by using what is rational as a benchmark, collectively we swing around it like a tetherball around a pole. That difference between rational decisions and real decisions is what we are going to call "The Insanity". The insanity includes all the little things we do that cause us to make less than optimal decisions, and there are plenty of them. That is the all the bad news for now, but we will expand upon it throughout the remainder of this book, so remember that you have something to look forward to.

The good news is that it is way more entertaining to read about the wacky antics that we get up to rather than a book about rational expectations. It is also not bad that over the past 50 or so years, researchers have started to make sense of these behaviors. Being able to identify the quirks in our decision-making processes has made them predictable, along with the influence each has on our

Market Insanity. DOI: 10.1016/B978-0-12-813115-2.00002-1

behaviors, including our investing behaviors. This has shaken-up behavioral science in a lot of ways, though not nearly as much as it has shaken investment markets, but before any of that will make any sense we need to have a crash course in some of the concepts and jargon hidden among these broad summaries.

There are two broad concepts here: First, that people act rationally, which is something that people have been trying way too hard to prove without much progress, leading to insanely complicated mathematical theorems and rules and assumptions that have gotten us nowhere. Second, since people act rationally, that markets must be efficient since people will respond to new information in a rational manner. The idea of market efficiency is a lot easier to explain because no one in their right mind looks at the stock market and believes for a moment they can realistically defend efficiency within it. So, the efficient market remains an assumption in which people, even today, continue to have faith; so they build their calculations of future market value, and making their investing decisions based on this assumption.

The idea of rationality, itself, is really old and a reasonable assumption if considered only briefly. It seems safe to assume that people are capable of making decisions that are in their best interest (Spoiler alert: How many people do you know that have made self-destructive or otherwise dumb decisions? Exactly). Sometime during the Enlightenment period of one country or another, the idea of rationality was officially declared boring by the general public after it was formalized by academics into a set of principles called Rational Choice Theory. Ignoring all the stuff that we do not care about for this book, rational choice theory states two simple thing: First, than given the choice between several viable options, they will either have a preference for 1, or be indifferent between 2 or more. Second, that if a person prefers option A over option B, and prefers option B over option C, then it must maintain that the person prefers option A over option C. Already we are running into a variety of problems, because both these statements about rational choice theory are bogus, but we will get into that in a minute.

Under the assumption that people are rational, it was long held that they are "utility maximizing agents", which is the way that economists say that people are able to recognize what will give them the most value, and will use the resources available to them in order to maximize that value. "Econ-Speak" is a language developed by economists to make simple statements sound super fancy, so let me clarify what that means. An "Agent" just refers to a person who is making a decision. They might be making it for themselves, or while representing an organization, but it is just a way to refer to any person making a choice. "Maximizing" is exactly what it sounds like: Taking something to its maximum possible value. "Utility" is simply the degree of usefulness that something has for an individual. A hammer will have far more utility for a carpenter than it would for a florist. Note that the amount of resources a person has available to them does matter when it comes to utility maximization, and that as you acquire more of a thing, it will provide you with less added utility every time.

The example I use for every class I have taught and every book I have written on this is the trade-off between beer and pizza. If you have $20 and you want to maximize your utility for the evening then you have to be rational about it. That first slice of pizza is amazing, and the ice cold beer that comes with it is even better. Since you are not so hungry anymore, the second slice of pizza is still pretty good but does not serve to be quite as useful as the first. So, you decide to buy 3 more beers, each seeming to increase in utility at ever-greater rates because you have a good buzz going, but that is a total illusion caused by being drunk. Suddenly it becomes quite apparent that the last beer you drank actually had negative utility because the room starts spinning and before you lose all the utility you gained over the evening, you quickly buy one more slice of pizza, because now pizza has a whole ton of utility to sop-up some of that alcohol and prevent you from becoming ill. By the end of the evening, you have racked-up a bill worth exactly $20, and you are so proud of yourself because you maximized your utility every step of the way, except now you do not have the money to provide a tip, so the people at the restaurant think you stiffed them, and you will not get optimal service next time you go out, somewhat lessening the total utility you achieved with $20.

That example is fantastic because it illustrates basic concepts of maximizing utility, the law of diminishing marginal returns (where you get less utility for every additional unit), the marginal rate of substitution (where you have so much of product A that the utility has gone down, and now product B has more utility), and exactly how fluid the concept of utility really is, making it utterly useless except in the most basic manner. In order to try and help it make sense, economists even went as far as to invent an imaginary unit of measurement for this called the "Util"! I kid you not, it is a real thing, and it serves no purpose at all so nobody actually uses it except in overly complicated mathematical modeling of philosophical concepts. For the majority of the global population – those who live in reality – utility is measured financially. If a person is willing to pay more for something, then that object must have more utility for them (this assumption is also bogus, but I promise we will discuss that later). This is where Paul Samuelson comes into the game. He recognized that the idea of utility maximization had merit, but that it was too abstract to ever be empirically used to develop a utility function – it could not be applied to the real world. His answer to this problem was to develop what he called "revealed preference". Basically, he said that to make utility maximization useful, it must be observed. The idea was that you would watch what people buy, and if they buy a thing then it must have utility for them. The rest of the world responded with "No shit"; that is to say, they were less than impressed. First of all, simply because a person is buying something, all it means is that it has utility for them; you do not know what they are giving-up in exchange, so there is no way to assess the comparative degrees of utility for different purchases. Second, if a person has no preference between the available options – if they have equal utility – then the choice will be made at random, and that is completely useless. Third, once you apply utility maximization to the real world, you do end-up with problems. It might be the case that Item A has more utility than Item B, and Item B has more utility than Item C, but it is totally possible that Item C has more utility than Item A. How can this be? Well, consider the last time you went car shopping. Imagine that the traits you are looking for are Price, Safety, and Speed. Car A has a good price and it is very safe, while Car B is a good price and it is fast but it is has a terrible safety record. Since you enjoy living, you decide that Car A is the better choice. Car C, on the other hand, is both very fast and very safe, but it is expensive as hell, and you decide that Car B is superior to Car C. On the other hand, Car C is not so much more expensive than Car A, but it is a lot faster, so you are willing to pay a little more if you can get the safety of Car A and the Speed of Car B. You have run into the problem of A > B, B > C, C > A.

That is not to say Samuelson was not onto something in trying to improve upon utility maximization, he just missed the mark on how to go about doing it. His ideas evolved into methods of assessing competitive price systems, developed in parallel to mathematical game theory-based theories of how markets reach equilibrium, and all that good stuff. Utility was just still kind of a useless concept. At best, revealed preference did not function much differently than utility maximization, and his application of utility gave it no more usefulness than as a synonym for "production"; such as when buying a machine – the revenues generated from the total output of the machine over its lifetime is the machine's total utility, which is just total revenues generated. Divide that by the cost of the machine and you have calculated the return on investment of purchasing that machine. That is ancient news, though – something which had been known way before Samuelson. So, revealed preference still had no more real world application than utility maximization. All he did was put a dollar sign on it.

Samuelson's efforts did inspire Sydney Afriat, who is credited with developing the set of parameters necessary to determine whether or not someone's purchases are consistent with utility maximization. Called Afriat's Theorem, it establishes 3 parameters which must be met to determine whether purchasing decisions have maximized utility. They are pretty complicated and not all that relevant to the book, so we will not go into the gritty details, but suffice it to say there have been many proofs that it functions properly. The question then became, "So what?" It comes back, once again to that deeper discussion of theoretical calculations and whether or not it is useful in the slightest. This is a matter which, as I write this, is still hotly debated, with both sides failing to make fully substantial arguments, for the most part. There are two arguments which stand-out, however, which demonstrate irrefutably that Afriat's Theorem, while functional, is rather pointless in the end, and that utility maximization functions will have little application to the real world. The first argument is that there have still been no applied utility function or beneficial use for Afriat's Theorem which does not rely on weak statistical models (i.e.: if you fudge anything enough, you will always get the answer you want). The second argument, and the most conclusive, comes from Herbert Simon, who coined the term "bounded rationality". Simply put, empirical observation is clear: people will never have all the information they need, the mental faculties to process all that information, or the time necessary to process all that information. In other words, there are limitations on what we are capable of processing, and people simply are not busting-out complex Theorems to determine whether they are maximizing their utility or not. It does not happen. Ever. To be quite frank, the vast majority of this book is nothing more than descriptions of the different ways our brains fail us as we try to remain rational, proven in theory and applied successfully to practical application. So, while the rationalists debate themselves into outdated obscurity, we have bigger things to worry about.

Do not misunderstand – behavioral economists are concerned with what is rational, too, because that is used as a sort-of an imaginary benchmark for the perfect decision. It is a bit like someone trying to live up the standards of Gilgamesh – it is a story told time and again with variations, no singular version being the definitively "correct" version, and trying to live up to that standard is impossible, but we can still develop some idea of just how epically we have failed. Every time we identify a new way that we are screwing things up, we get a little bit closer to understanding why we suck, and that gives us the opportunity to develop methods that help us suck a little less.

As applied to investing in the stock market (you were starting to think we would never get to it, admit it), this illusory rational perfection takes the form of a simple equation called the Capital Asset Pricing Model: $r_s = r_f + \beta(r_m - r_f)$. This say simply that the value of a specific asset is equal to the value of the risk-free rate (as defined by the interest rates paid by short-term government debt investments at any given point) plus an adjustment for the amount of risk being incurred by investing in something risky instead of a risk free investment. If an investment is extra risky, then it must be able to pay extra returns if it is going to attract investors away from the risk-free rate. If an investment is only a little risky, then it only needs to generate returns a little bit higher than the risk-free rate to attract investors. While this sounds great, like the idea of the rational consumer, the rational investor is a myth. The Capital Asset Pricing Model is Gilgamesh – a story that teaches us a few things but is functionally worthless. There are lots of different types of risk, and lots of ways to measure each type, and everyone has their own way to measure it, as well as their own way to respond to it. The same holds true for the value of an investment; lots of different types, lots of measurements of each type, and lots of ways people respond to it. Even if everyone agreed exactly on risk and returns, then they would still disagree on how high the returns must be in order to make it worth taking the risk, and even if everyone agreed on that, there is an entire book's worth of ways people screw it all up for themselves (which is great, because it keeps me employed).

So, we strive, and we strive, and we strive some more; ever trying to achieve the impossible, but improving a little more each time. The equations are still based loosely on the ideal rational CAPM concept, but they no longer resemble the original even in the slightest. They have evolved into complex monstrosities based on a more malleable equation built on something called Arbitrage Pricing Theory: $\mathbf{r}_s = \mathbf{r}_f + \beta_1 \mathbf{r}_1 + \beta_n \mathbf{r}_n$. Note that the value of a specific investment is still related to the risk-free rate, but instead of assuming a simplistic premium for a broad assessment of risk, it allows analysts to incorporate any number of factors in any way they want, even connecting separate equations together, and doing the most intricate things mathematics has available to try and become wealthy.

The underlying difference between Capital Asset Pricing Model and Arbitrage Pricing Theory is the assumption of the efficient market hypothesis. If investors are rational, then markets will necessarily be efficient. A rational investor will fully understand new information as soon as it is available, and adjust their investment portfolio in a manner that optimizes its returns using the Capital Asset Pricing Model. If investors were rational, though, then stocks would never be overvalued or undervalued, the market would not have bubbles and crashes, and none of the other things which we see on a daily basis which completely contradict the very idea that investors are acting rationally. No, the market is not efficient in the slightest, and that is why Arbitrage Pricing Theory was developed; even the word "arbitrage" refers to the process of finding investments which are mispriced and then profiting from the corrections which occur. If a stock's market price is lower than its value, then the price will eventually increase, and hopefully your custom-designed deluxe Value Model X3000 (with heated seats) will have picked-up on that and you will profit from the increase in market price. If a stock's market price is too high, then there are things you can do to profit from it going down, as well, but those moves are trickier and this is not a book about how to make investments. If you want that, you will have to go buy one of my books on finance, or ideally both of them (great gifts for the family, too!). So, the point of the all these customized equations which estimate the "true value" of a stock compared to its market price and then predict how the market price of the stock will change over time. Of course, no one has perfected it. The market average indices still beat-out even the savviest traders in the long-run. Very slowly we are getting better at it, though. We strive and we strive and we strive and continuously get just a little bit closer to becoming Gilgamesh…or becoming rational…. Either way you have accomplished something incredible.

The single largest advance in recent history was the discovery of behavioral influences on investor decisions. It began simply enough when economists realized that the markets were moving in ways that simply could not be explained by any rational analysis, while in the field of psychology important advances were being made into the manner in which people make decisions. These fields quickly merged and soon we have viable and reliable explanations for how our own behaviors were causing these irrational movements in the markets. Specifically, economist Robert Shiller debunked the efficient market hypothesis in 1981 when he published a study that evaluated stock market movements since the 1920s, and proved that the degree and timing of volatility in the market, and variations in the amount of volatility in the market, could not be wholly explained by any measure of rational expectations, whether it be changes in dividend policies, expectations of future earnings, or anything else. He did similar work in the real estate markets, and the result of all this was that his work absolutely decimated the efficient market hypothesis and, as by extension, the very idea that investors behave rationally. By incorporating psychological works that came before that study, and after that study, explanations for what was causing these changes in the market became apparent: It was not anything normal, quite to the contrary it was a thing most abnormal – it was us! Our brains! The things our brains make us do that are not good for us!

This research is all really new stuff, so investors are only now just barely starting to incorporate behavioral factors into their estimates of value and risk. They are starting to look at how investors behave and respond to the things they are exposed to, how they feel and the overall sentiment, the way people think and the odd ideas they have, and even the way people perceive what is real. Little by little these things are being incorporated into the calculations, slowly improving our ability to make them accurate; slowly allowing us to adjust for our own irrationality. If you are reading this, and I assume you are if you are seeing these words, then odds are you already know there is a difference between causation and correlation. Most of these studies are based on correlation, and have difficulty defining causation. There has been some progress in this area through the use of medical brain scanning technology and the involvement of neurologists, but most of the work still remains outside the realm of our ability to claim causation. Sure, we can be 99% certain, or 99.9% certain, but until the exact mechanism for the relationship is identified and clearly observed, we will still have to concede that there is some tiny chance that the relationship is being caused by some other factor. Is it possible that we are rational? Think of all the things which are almost certainly never going to happen in your lifetime – winning the lottery, getting hit by lightning, your winning lottery ticket getting fried by a lightning bolt – those are all more likely that the odds of you being rational.

As of now, emphasis in the research and application of stock investing is still placed on matters found within the rational paradigm. There is still quite a lot of knowledge to be taken from that area, but there is now a broad acceptance and enthusiasm for the behavioral paradigm, as well. Universities are starting to build their own behavioral economics programs and research centers (call me if you are looking for an early adopter and expert in the field, huh, guys?), and the amount of resources being dedicated to investor behavior rather than rational expectations has shifted dramatically, and will soon favor the behavioral paradigm. This is the pursuit of humanity, whether through physics or finance, we seek to better understand ourselves. It is through studies in behavioral investing that we come to better understand some of our greatest quirks and the effects they have which cause us to use our resources less efficiently. We are now incorporating these quirks into our equations, attempting to measure our own insanity with dollars and cents, giving us a benchmark for how close we, as a people, are to being rational. The funny thing is, though, that these efforts, in themselves, are a form of investing behavior. The pursuit of improving our estimates of value, our portfolio management strategies, and so forth, all comes from the psychological drive to improve our investing behaviors and earn more money. So, as we behave to better understand and correct our own insanity, and find ways to adjust our equations to account for our own psychological quirks, we have found a state that is sort-of rationally irrational.

Chapter 3

Bizarre Biases

Imagine for a moment that you are constantly surrounded by thousands of hallucinatory bureaucrats, accountants, salespeople, and artists, and they are all trying desperately to claw over each other to shove their own unique information in your face. They never go away, constantly screaming at you to get you to pay attention to them as they all push through an ever-larger and more aggressive crowd. Many of these people contradict each other, fight each other, and some are even determined to try and trick you, but no matter what you do, it goes-on every moment of every day. For your entire life... it never ends...the imaginary people shouting at you and shoving things directly into your face never go away. This is the world around you.

That is ok, though, because you have, at your disposal, a most amazing secretary. Within your brain there are bits which function to sort through all the information being thrown at you and decide what gets your attention. Not only that, but it will try to sort that information and put it in the correct context, summarize it to you in a way that makes it useful, and even show from where that information is attributed. Unfortunately, the secretary that lives in your brain has some problems dealing with more complex tasks, like those associate with investing activities. It is not that there is the occasional error, although those do occur from time to time, but rather that there are some systematic flaws in the way the information is handled, which we call biases. In other words, your mental secretary – in their attempt to help you – sometimes oversteps boundaries. Generally speaking, a bias is any flaw in the way we process the information around us, leading us to faulty conclusions. There can be all sorts of biases, and in the stock market we tend to see all of them, although in this book we will focus on a few of the more entertaining.

3.1 SELF-SERVING BIAS

Strongly related to narcissism, it is all too common to see self-serving bias on Wall Street. Simply put, people tend to give themselves credit for a success, but blame something else for a failure. The result is that people tend to repeat their mistakes, and when the same problem arises again and again, sometimes the person will go as far as to invent some kind of imaginary structural injustice in which they are perpetually the victim, or in some extreme cases might even develop a paranoia of people creating conspiracies against them. In those who are already more prone to being mentally unstable, it is entirely possible for these

Market Insanity. DOI: 10.1016/B978-0-12-813115-2.00003-3

15

paranoias to develop even when the mistakes are being made by someone close to them. For example, in an interview with the Wall Street Journal conducted by Michael Bender on March 14, 2017, White House counselor Steve Bannon describes the events which led to his extreme and bizarre behaviors. According to Bannon, his father made some poor investing decisions prior to the 2008 financial crisis in response to advice from a television financial correspondent. Rather than accept his father was responsible for his own actions, in fact failing to consult with Steve, himself, who was working at Goldman Sachs at the time, Steve instead blamed the media. That is the story according to Steve, but it is what comes next that is truly bizarre and demonstrates how self-serving bias can easily turn into a full-blown psychotic paranoia. Steve did not just blame the financial correspondent or the television station for which he worked, Steve blamed the entirety of all media, creating within his own mind a mass conspiracy in which all media was portraying lies to manipulate average, working-class Americans like his father. The first red flag should have been when he quit his job at Goldman Sachs and purchased the conspiracy website Breitbart, heavily promoting it and using it as an outlet for his anti-media crusade. Oddly enough, this crusade eventually landed him a job working with a US President until he was fired for his bizarre behaviors, yet the manner in which a simple investment-oriented self-serving bias exploded quickly into a delusional paranoia necessary to sustain the bias resulted in behaviors which are generally considered to be self-destructive. This type of extreme example is rare, however.

The more moderate forms of self-serving bias are extremely common. For example, pay attention to the statements made by the executive management of corporations; when a company is doing well, they are more than happy to accept huge bonuses and apply the success to the strategies or changes they implemented within the company. When a company has annual losses, though, the executives still tend to get bonuses – even if they are fired, they generally get bonuses which have come to be known as a "golden parachute" – and the blame will be placed on changes in the market or a general economic downturn. Executives at corporate banks during the 2008 Financial Collapse would typically blamed other individuals within the company for illegal or faulty contracts, stating that the signature approving the contract was placed by rubber stamp. Well, that still puts the executive at fault for approving the use of the rubber stamp. There is a common saying, crude though true, that "shit rolls downhill" meaning that blame for failure is placed at the lowest level of authority possible, despite the tendency for everyone possible trying to take credit for success. So, why is it that successes are not attributed to economic improvements, and failures attributed to the inability of management to adapt to changes in the market? It is more than simply trying to avoid a criminal record, because people do truly believe in the success of one's self and the failure of another. It all comes-down to the self-serving bias.

Professional investors do this sort of thing all the time. They will believe that any successful investments they made were the inevitable result of their own genius, while financial losses were the unforeseeable fault of corporate manage-ment, government regulation, economic conditions, or some other matter. By blaming some external factor, they are not only failing to correct their own fail-ures, but they then make future investing decisions based partly in response to whatever it is they blamed despite that thing being completely irrelevant (or at least misapplied) to their previous losses, making it even more likely that they will make more mistakes in the future. Not only did they fail to recognize the true source of the mistake, but they are now incorporating faulty information into their future decisions.

Take a good look at yourself. How many times has something bad happened, major or minor, and you tried to justify that it was unavoidable when you know damn well you saw it coming a mile away? How many times have you done something you knew was dumb but you hesitantly did it anyway because some-one told you it would be fine? The fault was not theirs – if they were so confident it was a good idea they would have been doing it, themselves. Instead they con-vinced you to do it, despite the fact that you knew better. The frequency with which you do this depends on who you are, so who are you? According to a 1977 study by James Larson, you are more likely to exhibit self-serving bias if you have high self-esteem, if you are in a good mood, or if you have an ex-ternal locus of control. Simply put, your brain is going to try to defend itself against threats to your self-image or your emotional state, and that is particu-larly easy to do if you have a tendency to believe that events are outside of your control.

So what can you do about it? It is not your fault that you are amazing and feeling great about it, right? So how can you avoid self-serving bias in your investing decisions? The solution might sound like some cheesy motivational workshop, but if you want to limit the effects of self-serving bias then you need to take time before and after you make a decision. Before you make a decision, identify specifically those factors you can control and those you cannot. After you make a decision, force yourself to identify things you did well, and things you could have done better. Even if it was a failure, write-down some things you did well that prevented the result from being worse; and even if it was a success, write-down some things you could have done better to improve the results even more. Once you have done that, take those lessons and use them the next time a similar decision arises, but do not dwell on either your successes or your failures.

3.2 STATUS QUO BIAS

People can be really resistant to change. Not only will people endure suffering and failure through common justifications as "Better the Devil you know, than the Devil you do not", but people will sometimes become verbally and physi-cally violent when pressured into accepting a change in those things they have become comfortable with. The problem is that uncertainty leads to fear of the unknown, and it is just in the nature of change that there is a degree of uncertainty to it. The simple fact is that since we have not experienced the new, we cannot be fully certain of its nature, and that can cause anxiety in people triggering the "fight/flight/freeze" reflex. Even when things are going poorly and there is a chance for improvement, a lot of people will opt to keep things the same out of the risk that the change will cause things to become worse. They have adapted and accepted the current circumstances, and are afraid to disrupt the status quo. Hence, we get something called the status quo bias.

The majority of the research on status quo bias focuses on retirement accounts, pensions, and other mediums through which people invest in mutual funds and/or index funds. First by Samuelson and Zeckhauser in 1988 on Harvard pension plans; then by Patel, Zeckhauser, and Hendricks throughout the 1990s studying fund investments; then in the early 2000s, several different teams started looking at the tendency to buy individual stocks rather than funds, including Ameriks and Zeldes in 2001; then Barber, Odean, and Zhu in 2003; and finally circling around to research on hedge fund investments by Agarwal, Daniel, and Naik in 2004. So in 2005 when Kempf and Ruenzi redid the pension experiments originally done by Samuelson and Zeckhauser, they were really kicking a dead horse, and every one of these team always came to the same conclusion: People will choose investments they have chosen before, or which they already hold, even if there are clearly superior options available.

It is a bit preposterous to think about a person being given two options and picking the worse one just because it is familiar. Why this occurs so consistently in the financial sector is yet unknown. You do not see people with chronic diseases refusing new cures just because they have gotten used to the idea of being sick, so why would a person intentionally choose an investment option that underperforms compared to the alternative? Suggestions include that it may be related to the endowment effect (which is discussed in Chapter 5.2), so that people place greater value on what they already own. Oddly enough, the research also shows that the amount of status quo bias we tend to exhibit is related to the number of potential options available; when you have more options, you are more likely to stick with what you have. Perhaps the sense of being overwhelmed increases the anxiety associated with change, which is reasonable. There is a related phenomenon called "Choice Overload" (a term coined by Alvin Toffler in the book Future Shock), in which people simply fail to make a decision because there are more possible options than they can mentally process. In the absence of choice, the status quo would be the default decision. Still, that does not explain the experiments which have been done wherein people are given as few as 2 available options. Still having a hard time wrapping your brain around why someone might behave this way? You are not the only one, but it is easy to criticize when you are reading about it, and an entirely different matter when you are faced with the decision, yourself (which would be a really cool experiment using virtual reality, but potentially cause serious psychological distress as people witness the traumatic deaths of others). So, what can you do to limit status quo bias in your own decisions? There are 3 recommendations I will make in this book:

1) If you are faced with a large number of options and are feeling over-whelmed, stop looking at the individual options and think of them in terms of categories. Exactly what are you looking for in an investment that meets your goals? That will allow you to limit the large percentages of the choices available by simple process of elimination. The more specific you can be with what you want, the more options you will be able to eliminate, making your decision much simpler.

2) There is a process in change management that is called Lewin's 3-Stage Model of Change. Simply put, you start by looking critically at the reasons the status quo is flawed. Do not just ignore them, really do the calculations to see exactly what you are missing by staying the course. Then, once you are ready, make your decision. If you decided to change your investment – to stray from the status quo – then keep track of your new investments to see how much better you are doing compared to your previous position.

3) You can trick your own brain through something called the "mere exposure effect". First discovered by Gustav Fechner in 1876, this has been a windfall for marketing firms around the world. The premise is simple: The more you are exposed to something, the more you will tend to like it. You might know this concept better as "acquired taste". Have you ever heard a song that you hated at first, but as you heard it over and over again you could not help but start to enjoy it? What about the taste of a particular drink or food which at first seemed disgusting but something about it kept drawing you back until you found yourself enjoying it? Well, by simply taking some extra time to study an alternative investment, and expose yourself more to the details, what you are actually doing is fooling your brain into accepting the alternative investment as being part of the status quo by using the mere exposure effect.

3.3 CONFIRMATION BIAS

There is a hypothesis which exists, best illustrated by a team at Carnegie Mellon University featured in 2003 which states that the brain tends to function is a way that utilizes the least amount of effort. If you look closely at the people around you, then you just might find yourself enthusiastically agreeing with that hypothesis, but there is yet no hard evidence to support the claim. Still, if it is true, then it might help to explain why people tend to only pay attention and accept information that confirms what they think they already know. It takes a lot more effort to reject your old ideas about the way things are and replace them with new ones, and even more work to learn enough about the new ideas to logically and intelligently be able to change your mind on a particular matter. So people tend to either avoid or dismiss any information which contradicts what they think they know, and go so far as to dismiss information that does not inherently contradict their current knowledge set if it comes from a source they have rejected as being inherently contradictory. That means people give all their attention only to that information which confirms their preconceived notions, which is why this form of bias is called confirmation bias.

Confirmation bias has been well-known and documented even before it was given a formal name, and before any formal study of the mind, itself. The earliest known reference to it comes from roughly the year 400 BCE by Greek historian Thucydides who wrote, "It is a habit of mankind to entrust to careless hope what they long for, and to use sovereign reason to thrust aside what they do not fancy". Though it was Dante Alighieri in The Divine Comedy who may more accurately have observed that "Affection for one's own opinion binds, confines the mind", as this would tie the types of confirmation bias and its consequences together more neatly, even perhaps going as far as to relate confirmation bias to status quo bias (discussed in Chapter 3.2). We are getting ahead of ourselves, though. Confirmation bias was first proved as a psychological phenomenon by Klayman and Ha in 1987, in a study that utilized Bayesian probability by having participants try to estimate about the rules which determine the pattern in a series of numbers, and then determining whether they would deviate from their current hypothesis in subsequent questions using preconceived ideas, or informed assessments of the current question. Sure enough, the bias was confirmed. Never bet against people making dumb decisions.

Since then, we have been able to identify 3 ways in which confirmation bias occurs:

1) Biased acceptance of information: People will intentionally expose themselves exclusively to sources of information they like. This has a strange doubled-effect in that not only does the individual expose themselves only to information which confirms what they already believe (or want to believe), but also in that they are more willing to accept new information from these sources. By contrast, if they are exposed to information that contradicts their beliefs, or new information is coming from a source which contradicts their own favored sources, then that information will be automatically rejected. In extreme cases, the emotional dedication to a source of information takes precedence, and even if that source of information contradicts itself, a person will believe in both contradicting sets of information in a state that is known as "cognitive dissonance". In order to maintain that cognitive dissonance, some people will do mental gymnastics that deserve an Olympic gold medal, generally requiring the use of a variety of logical fallacies, and good ol' plain denial. This makes confirmation bias similar to status quo bias in that people are holding-on to their existing beliefs and are not will prevent themselves from even being exposed to information which contradicts those beliefs, entirely denying anything which violates the status-quo in their brain.

2) Biased interpretation of information: This is more commonly known as "spin", which is frequently done inadvertently, but far too often it is actually

a concerted effort to gain support for a particular assertion by some asshole trying to manipulate people. Do not think for a moment all the financial experts on TV or on the internet are telling you the truth in an objective, unbiased manner. In fact, some have been caught red-handed taking advantage of their position as a public figure, and have been required to sign contracts stating that they cannot trade in investments they have discussed publicly for a number of months or else they will get fired, with the potential for criminal prosecution for stock market manipulation. In either case, a person may look at information and draw completely inappropriate or incorrect conclusions from it. They may frame the information in a manner that cherry-picks just the parts they want to believe, or they may apply subjective opinions or unproven assertions to make the information fit a particular belief, or they may apply any of a number of logical fallacies. The biased interpretation of information contributes greatly to the polarization of opinion, given that two people may look at the exact same information and draw separate conclusions, with at least one of those people drawing improper conclusions.

3) Biased recollection of information: Memory is a funny thing. Even if you avoid bias in your acceptance and interpretation of information, there is a chance you will selectively forget those things which contradict your opinion. Humans have a tendency to hold onto memories they like more strongly than memories they do not like. In fact, particularly traumatic memories will sometimes be altered in the brain to dull the visceral and psychological reaction we have to them, editing either the severity or details of the event (as a side note of interest, this is a phenomenon that is currently being explored by psychologists for use in treatment of PTSD in soldiers, often with the assistance of virtual reality simulations or experimental mind-altering pharmaceuticals). So naturally, if a person is prone to having a confirmation bias, then they will more readily recollect those memories of information which help them to maintain that bias. This contributes to a related phenomenon called the irrational primacy effect, in which a person will favor the information they received first, rather than any information they receive at a later time that contradicts the beliefs they originally constructed. Since a person will construct a belief about something based on their first exposure to information about a particular assertion, everything that comes after that moment will be assessed in comparison to the first exposure, and confirmation bias makes us more prone to remembering a lineage of information which maintains consistency, rather than remembering that information which contradicts our original assessments. Once again, this shows evidence for a relationship between confirmation bias and status quo bias, as a result of a person applying an irrational primacy and recollecting only those things which support that irrationality.

Those are the types of confirmation bias, and although there are three distinct types, they all have the same impact on your financial decisions, and the news is not good. According to books by Hilton (2001), Pompian (2006), and Krueger and Mann (2009), the studies have shown that confirmation bias can devastate your investment portfolio for two primary reasons. First and foremost, confirmation bias results in an investor just completely rejecting information that could be vital to their investing decisions. When investing, information that contradicts your beliefs is far more important than information which validates them. After all, if your investing decisions are already going to be based on your existing beliefs, then new information that simply validates those beliefs are of no consequence, but new information that challenges your beliefs provides opportunities to change the decisions you make and improve upon what you would have previously decided. So to ignore such information is among the greatest follies an investor can make, but to make matters even worse, as an investor continues to find information that confirms their beliefs, they will become ever more confident in their strategies and decisions. Why should they since everything they are seeing is confirming just how amazing they are? This overconfidence leads to decreased risk aversion, causing a person to take unnecessarily high risk in an investment or investment strategy which is already based on biased and incomplete information. Overall, this all makes you one hell of a terrible investor.

The source of confirmation bias is not certain. It might be as simple as a matter of personal insecurity. A lot of people do not like to be wrong, and will even deny being wrong when presented with irrefutable evidence to the contrary to avoid looking foolish to others, or feeling foolish, themselves. No matter the reason for confirmation bias, though, there are a few tricks you can use to help avoid making these mistakes. In a 2009 article in the Wall Street Journal written by Jason Zweig entitled How to Ignore the Yes-Men in your Head makes recommendations such as making the assumption that your investments or strategies have already failed, and exploring possible reasons that such a thing may have occurred. Other methods include mental exercises like Devil's Advocate, in which you actively seek-out alternate beliefs and use them to argue against your own position in order to see whether you can properly defend it. Use of the Socratic Method can also be useful, wherein any assertion you make or belief you hold is questioned incessantly like a petulant child who will not stop asking "Why?" If you do not know the answer to your own ideas and beliefs, then clearly you do not have the information you need to make an informed decision based upon it, and need to reconsider your position.

3.4 STATISTICAL BIAS

This is sort-of the oddball of the biases being included in this book because it does not result from humans acting like oddballs, it could just as easily be the result of simply screwing-up the data you are analyzing in some way. There are several behaviors which result in statistical bias, each unique in their own way, but the end result is always the same: your calculations will be wrong and the investments you make based on those calculations will be crap (or if the investments you make are good, you will still have made them for crappy reasons). To be more specific, all types of statistical bias share a single commonality that defines them as statistical biases – they are actions which result in the systematic error of the sampled data from reality. In other words, something has happened which is causing your analytics to be consistently higher or consistently lower than they should be, and you need to reconsider the methods you are using.

Normally, and ideally, this portion of the book would get all sorts of mathy, with lots of equations describing how estimators can systematically deviate from parameters regardless of variance and standard deviation, but luckily for you I cannot do that at the moment. Besides, books that get too mathy do not sell very well unless they are part of a required college course. So, instead of explaining the actual mechanics of statistical bias, we will just talk about how it causes people to deviate from rational investing decisions, contributing to the insanity.

The first source of statistical bias, and the only one people tend to remember if they took 1 or 2 statistics courses in college, is sampling bias. This one can be easily explained with an example. Let us say you want to collect data on equities in the clothing retailer market, but for reasons you cannot seem to explain, all the data you collected came from the annual reports of lingerie retailers only, completely ignoring all other types of clothing retailers. As a result, your sample data does not represent the total market for clothing retailers because you only focused on a single specific niche within that market, rather than the market as a whole, and you get fired for being completely inept as a financial analyst. In short, sampling bias results when the sample you collect is not representative of the population. There are a number of stock indices which attempt to capture specific segments of the stock market, such as the Dow Jones Transportation Average, which is a sample of 20 large corporations within the transportation sector, including airlines, railroads, delivery services, and things of that nature. If this sample of the transportation sector focused only on passenger transportation, then they would be forgetting entirely about some of the largest transportation companies in the world that deal exclusively in shipping cargo by land, sea, and air. Such an index flawed in this manner could only result from sampling bias.

The 2nd source of statistical bias we will discuss is so broad in its nature that it encompasses a wide range of other, more specific, sources of bias, so this is also the last source of statistical bias we will cover in this book. Formally known as "Estimator bias", you can avoid a lot of jargon by thinking about it merely as flaw in some benchmark being used to perform data analysis. A great example of estimator bias could be found in the banking sector prior to the 2008 financial collapse (which really began in October 2007, but who are we to second-guess those who give popular names to such events?). To all but the most astute, the banking sector seemed to be doing fantastic – prime investment material. They were issuing record numbers of loans that would generate the kind of revenue growth that makes any professional investor drool with anticipation. The analytics that are regularly used were completely sound, and the conclusions which were drawn valid based upon those analytics. The problem was that the analytics used assumed normal operational and financial performance, while the reality was that the quality of the loans being issued had dropped significantly. Banks always face the reality that a small percentage of their loans will not be repaid, but what they did not disclose was that this percentage was skyrocketing. For investors, the result was that data analysis which would have otherwise been completely legitimate no longer represented reality because of a change in the conditions of the population they were sampling. Their analyses painted a picture that was consistently too positive – too hopeful. Had they known the population of the banking sector was experiencing a decrease in the quality of their revenue streams, then the investors could have adjusted accordingly.

This banking example is a particular type of estimator bias called the "omitted variable bias". Unfortunately for investors, this is a bias that is completely unavoidable. We will never have all the information we need, and even if such a thing was physically possible (which it is not), then it would most certainly be prohibitively expensive and time-consuming. This is a matter that will be discussed in greater detail in Chapters 4.5 and 4.6, though. In the meantime, let us move-on to how a type of bias you can never escape will inevitably destroy your investment portfolio, sealing your fate! Or not. Maybe there is a solution. Keep reading to find out.

Problem = Incorrect data collection and analysis results in inappropriate investment decisions. That is really the long and short of it. If you start with crappy information, then you are going to make crappy decisions. Simple enough, eh? Once again, the real problem here is that you are doomed to start with crappy information. That is why index funds consistently outperform managed funds. So what can possibly be done to prevent yourself from making crappy decisions?

Solutions = You have two options: The difficult but highly valuable choice, and the simple choice that does not really tell us anything useful (yet has helped statisticians around the world to cut corners!). The more difficult option is to do the thorough research necessary to identify systematic flaws you are currently experiencing, do more research to identify factors which play a role in the market price of investments or the market as a whole, and incorporate that new information into your investing strategies. It is a long and tedious process, but it is one that actually answers questions and provides useful information that can be applied and built-upon, improving human understanding of our own investing behaviors. Truly, it is a noble cause, and one that I am happy to perform for the right price (hint, hint). If you are not so inclined to perform research, or pay someone else to do it for you, then there is an easier way. Statisticians have a factor represented by the Greek letter eta, which they tack onto the end of a wide range of equations, known as "error". This is essentially a catch-all factor that says, "My equation does not work exactly right and I do not know why, but we can mathematically adjust it to make it work." This only works in practice if the difference between your estimates and reality remain relatively constant. If that is the case, you can simply adjust your estimates by the difference in value to get the right answers. The problem is that since you do not know what is causing the error, you cannot do anything to predict if it will change. If you do not really know what is going-on, then even if your estimates are correct, your investments are still being made blindly, which is not ideal.

3.5 HOME BIAS

In the matter of investing in foreign stocks, people get complicated. Not only is there a bizarre puzzle associated with this, but also a functional paradox, and to top it all off, there is an inherent risk that was recently discovered that barely anyone knows about. First, let us keep things simple, though. The short explanation is that people prefer to invest in stocks which are domestic. Xu, Hu, and Fan (2009) confirmed that the amount of difference between cultures plays a role in the amount of investments made between those countries, with nations of greater cultural difference investing less in each other than nations with more similar cultures. Baik, Kang, Kim, and Lee (2012) later confirmed this by demonstrating that both cultural differences and the amount of unfamiliarity investors have with a given culture reduce the degree to which they are willing to invest in nations with such cultures. In other words, no matter what country you live in, the people in that country will prefer to invest in equities from within that country. Maybe the familiarity gives a sense of comfort and reduced risk, maybe it is just simpler, or maybe we are all jingoist jerk who see foreign equities as inferior to our own. No one really knows, but whatever the reason is, we all need to get over it, because the only thing they are accomplishing is screwing-up their financial performance.

That is the puzzling thing. It has been proven that investment portfolios with international diversification tend to perform better than purely domestic portfolios. In a 2007 study by Karen Lewis, she demonstrated that increasing the ratio of foreign equities in an investment portfolio lowers volatility risk without compromising the quality of returns. There are two primary reasons for that. First, by going global, you are expanding the pool of potential investment targets. That is the fancy way of saying there are more stocks available for you to choose, and it is very likely you will find at least 1 or 2 that are better than you stick with 100% domestic stocks. The second reason international diversification helps portfolio performance is that it allows us to limit our exposure to systematic risk. There are lots of different types of risk, but when you are talking about diversification, we are really worried about two broad categories: specific and systematic. Specific risk is the risk that comes with any individual stock investment. The reason people buy a variety of different stocks rather than "putting all their eggs into one basket", so to speak, is that there is always a degree of uncertainty in any investment, and if a single investment fails then you want to make sure that you have your assets spread-out to limit the amount of loss. Systematic risk, on the other hand, is the risk that the entire stock market will crash, as is common during recessions. Even if a company has solid operational and financial performance, when a recession hits, the market price of all stocks tend to drop like a rock... tied to a somewhat larger rock. Fortunately, not all nations around the world experience recessions at the same time, so buying foreign stocks helps limit the amount of risk associated with the economy of a single nation. Still, despite better performance and a known explanation for those improvements, people are still averse to foreign equities.

That is where the paradox comes into play. If people are so averse to foreign investments, then how is it that for decades we have been seeing a dramatic increase in the cointegration of global stock markets? How is it that we can maintain home bias, yet continue to invest in foreign investments to the degree that our stock markets are influencing each other to ever-greater degrees? Until the mid-1990s, the correlation coefficient for market comovements remained steady at approximately 0.4, while they jumped to an amazing 0.9 between 1995 and 2005 (Saunders & Cornett, 2013). Shi, Bilson, Powell, and Wigg (2010) demonstrated that equity markets are particularly integrated between nations that have a high degree of foreign direct investment. We might be able to explain-away this paradox by simply stating that people are able to overcome their home bias in the pursuit of improved returns, but there is even a cost premium associated with foreign stocks. It was shown by Baik et al. (2012), that cultural differences and unfamiliarity with a given culture has a negative correlation with future returns, indicating that a cultural cost premium exists for foreign investments. These findings are supported by Christelis and Georgarakos (2013), which confirmed the existence of elevated entry costs for foreign investments as compared to domestic investments, leading investors to specialize in domestic equities as a result of decreased returns on foreign investments caused by the cost premium. So, not only are we faced with the contradictions that foreign equities have a cost premium yet internationally diversified portfolios outperform purely domestic portfolios, but investors remain particularly averse to foreign equities due to cost premiums and the unfamiliarity of "foreignness" despite strong indications that they are investing in each other's markets directly at a greater rate than ever.

To complicate things even further, there is validity to the risk aversion associated with the unfamiliar, or degree of foreignness associated with a particular nation and its equities. A study done by Taillard (yeah, me) in 2017 showed that there is a very strong and very consistent correlation between the degree of aversion investors in a particular country have to volatility, and the measure of cultural uncertainty avoidance in that nation. This correlation held constant not only over time between 1980 and 2010, but even using different frameworks of cultural uncertainty avoidance, measured using both the methodologies ap-

	1980 (Hofstede)	2004 (GLOBE)	2010 (Hofstede)
Volatility Risk	Alpha (0.374)* Partial Correlation	Beta (-0.363)** Spearman's Rho	Alpha (0.370)** Spearman's Rho Alpha (0.424)** Partial Correlation
Value Risk	P/E (-0.691)** Partial Correlation OCF/Share (-0.307)* Spearman's Rho	P/E (-0.193)* Partial Correlation	N/A

*p=0.05 **p=0.01
Red = No significant difference in the absolute values of the correlation coefficients using Fisher r-to-z

FIGURE 3.1   Results of Testing Cultural Influence on Equity Investor Risk Aversion

plied by Hofstede and the GLOBE initiative led by House. That means that even though people from different nations are looking at the exact same risk analytics data, the way they perceive risk between nations differs, so that the stock market in a foreign nation will not respond to volatility in the manner one might expect from their own domestic market. This means that metrics of value and risk will decrease in their accuracy and validity when applied to foreign markets, unless they are incorporating culture as a variable in their analyses. To reiterate, though, the cointegration of global stock markets has increased enough that differences in response to metrics of value risk have statistically been eliminated during the sample period, as shown in Fig. 3.1.

As a side note, the partial correlations performed held mean GDP growth rate over the previous 3 years constant as a proxy for investor sentiments, since confidence indices do not have available data in all the nations included, nor in all the year included.

I warned you that people get all sorts of complicated and confused when it comes to the matter of home bias. We have something of a love-hate relationship with foreign investments, but it does appear that we are slowly getting over the idea of foreignness as a barrier to investing. That does not stop us from acting like doofuses and applying a home bias to our decisions, though! To the contrary, a study performed in 1999 by Covas and Moskowitz demonstrated not that people prefer domestic firms, but they go so far as to show a preference for companies who are headquartered in the local area. Yeah, even among domestic firms, people tend to prefer investing in local companies, rather than domestic companies headquartered further away. The problems which arise from home bias are simple, and we have already discussed them, in a way. Earlier in this chapter we discussed how foreign diversification can help improve portfolio performance, well, to understand the problems that home bias causes we need only look at them in reverse. First of all, home bias eliminates our ability to diversify our portfolios in ways that limits systematic risk. If the economy has a recession and the stock market hits a low trough in the cycle, then someone with home bias is just going to have to find a way to ride that wave and hope they do not wipe-out. Second, having a home bias will cause you to look only at domestic investments, completely ignoring the majority of potential investments available around the world, many of which would likely perform better than what you are currently holding. Ok, so let us say you have some conscious ideological basis for investing only in domestic companies and are insistent only in investing in US companies. (I use the US as an example because based on my publisher's distribution and marketing strategy, odds are you are a US citizen if you are reading this book. If you are not from the US, then please do not feel left-out, because home bias applies to people of all nationalities, so you are likely just as bizarre in this respect as even the nuttiest of US investors!) The idea of "Invest American" does not just stop there, as already discussed – it easily becomes "Invest Michigan", which tends to naturally transition to "Invest in Detroit", but the whole ideology is just as dumb as if you were to limit it to a single city block with an investment strategy of "Invest at the Corner of Lahser rd and Fenkell rd!". The only thing you are actually accomplishing is continuing to increasingly limit the potential of your investments. You may feel some sort of pride in helping your hometown grow, but you are not going to help that happen by devastating your investment portfolio with bad investments. By broadening your options as much as possible, you can maximize the returns on your investments and then use your success to accomplish your ideological goals, but that cannot happen if you are broke.

So, what do you do to prevent home bias? Simply being aware that it is a thing is a good first step. You might be surprised how few people – even professional investors – are aware that it is a thing; people often do not even consider the possibility that they can invest abroad. Another thing you can do to avoid home bias is to analyze your potential investments without actually looking at the names. Perhaps use the "RAND" function in Excel to assign each company a random number as a code, that way you are not aware of the nationality of the company you are reviewing. Of course, after you have made your decisions, you would then need to reference the numbers you picked with the list of companies, and if some of those companies are foreign, it is then prudent to make adjustments in your analytics, as necessary. If you are a little more computer savvy, you can actually just include adjustments for national origin in your analytics, and run the program as normal. That way you are eliminating personal, subjective preference in companies, as compared to objective analytics. Of course, your analytics and algorithms could be completely wrong – if you do not know what you are doing, then none of this will help you except in the sense that it will help eliminate your home bias.

CONCLUSION

Whether we like to admit it or not, we all play favorites when it comes to investments. Maybe we blindly admire our own decisions as infallible, or maybe we like the way things are and want to keep it that way regardless of available alternatives, or maybe we favor only certain types of information, or maybe we have an egocentric view of the world and reject anything that is too different from ourselves. In the end, that is what biases are all about – playing favorites, even if it means that you are not making great investments as a result. These behaviors, most of them, are merely the result of how the brain functions – they are our default settings most of the time – but when we learn to overcome them and become just a bit more rational in our thinking, our approach to the market will improve.

Chapter 4

Bad Behavior

Oh yes, you have been naughty and we both know it, but that has nothing to do with this book. This chapter is not about deviance or seduction, it is a bit more literal than that: This chapter is about behaviors people exhibit, whether they realize it or not, which are not good for your investment portfolio. Oftentimes, even if you are aware of the behavior, it cannot be helped because you are left with no other option. Other times, you will not even be aware of what has happened, unless someone has pointed it out to you in hindsight – it is just hard-wired in your brain. Then, there are those times when a person is fully aware that what they are doing is not in their best interest, but they do it anyway because of reasons they often cannot even articulate which is the insanity inherent within us. Either way, the way you are behaving is preventing you from making ideal investment decisions, but thankfully that does not mean you need to get rid of that leather riding crop.

4.1 HERD BEHAVIOR

Arguably the most commonly-known type of investor behavior in existence. You have seen it on TV or in some movie before: The scene is a crowded room of people, most commonly the floor of a stock exchange but sometimes shown as an auction, when suddenly a single voice rings-out with a bid to purchase, triggering the entire room to suddenly erupt in a cacophony of desperately competing offers on the same transaction. While there was a time when this was not too far from the truth, the trading floor at stock exchanges are now quiet places filled with computer terminals and the occasional poor schmuck who could not work from his own office for some reason. That is not to say that herd behavior does not exist, though, as it is more prominent than ever; just by more inconspicuous means.

There are a variety of television shows and written media telling you how to invest; there are subscription services which allow you to watch the investments being made by one prominent investor or another so that you can follow-along and mimic their trades. These are just formal ways by which people who do not have the time or inclination or confidence to assess an investment for themselves will take cues from others.

There is a very deeply-rooted reason for this type of behavior that has evolved within our brains for nothing less than our very survival. Imagine for a moment that you are in a grassy or wooded area in Africa in about the year

Market Insanity. DOI: 10.1016/B978-0-12-813115-2.00004-5

100,000 BCE, hanging-out by a campfire and enjoying a refreshing beverage, when it comes to your attention that very nearby a large group of people are all running frantically in a single direction. You do not know why they are running, so if you are the type of person to wait there and find-out, odds are good that you will not be passing-on your genes to the next generation. If you are the type of person to join the group and find-out why you are all running, then you might just discover that you have joined a race, or you might discover that you have nearly missed being eaten by something with teeth bigger than your own, allowing your genes to pass to the next generation, making them also more prone to survival.

Rejoining the modern era, you are more likely to go bankrupt than you are to get eaten, so when you start to see stocks in a particular industry move consistently up or down, it is completely reasonable to think that the rest of the market knows something you do not, so chances are high you will follow their lead then try to learn why later. This was well-described by Grossman and Stiglitz in 1976, wherein they explain how uninformed investors will use market price as an alternative to actual information under the assumption that market price is based on a collection of rational decisions made by informed investors (those poor fools). It does not matter that it is a terrible idea to invest in an industry or a company so volatile that taking an extra day or two to do proper research will make all the difference, there is a deep fear of the unknown that urges us to follow the crowd, even if the rest of the crowd does not know what they are doing, either. There is substantial literature which attributes this phenomenon to investment bubbles; wherein investors see an upward trend in some sector, and then they will perpetuate that upward trend in stock price way beyond its sustainable level simply because each person will invest more. In other words, the price rises higher for no other reason than because investors see the price rising higher. Of course, herd behavior is difficult to quantify, making it difficult to objectively prove specific quantitative contributions to bubbles, but in Chapter 6.1 we will discuss another culprit contributing to investment bubbles.

Another contributing factor to herd behavior combines investor confidence (which will also be discussed in greater detail in Chapter 6.1), tendencies for people to conform to the social environment around them, and the contagious spread of mood (discussed in more detail in Chapter 6.1). Put simply, imagine 4 people in a car and the driver puts-on some corny pop music from the 1980s, and they start genuinely rocking to it so hard that you simply cannot help but feel some of their enthusiasm, and before you know it everyone in the car is acting like total fools but enjoying it, anyway. Well, the stock market is filled with fools ready to mirror back any enthusiastic sentiments, whether they are positive or negative.

To avoid herd behavior, the best thing you can do is simply avoid the herd. Unless the herding is related to investments you already own, do not bother yourself with it. You may feel like you are missing-out on something, but the only thing you would be missing is the information necessary to continue making informed decisions. Herd behavior is a little unique in that you can go a step beyond avoiding it, though. If you are savvy enough to identify herding or a bubble that is growing, you might consider a strategy in which you ride the herd for a short while to benefit from its momentum briefly before breaking away, or do the total opposite of the herd to take advantage of changes in market price. These strategies can be risky, though, because they attempt to make rational investments out of irrational behaviors, and that is not an easy thing to do.

4.2 ANCHORING

Here is a fun experiment you can do on your own. Take a deck of cards and remove all the face cards, leaving it as a deck of 1–10, then shuffle it. Show someone the top card, then ask them to guess how many dollars you have in your wallet. Now go do the exact same thing to someone else who did not see you try it the first time. Clearly, the card that the person sees is completely irrelevant – it is random, and has nothing to do with the amount of money in your wallet. If you do this enough times, though, you will notice that people who see cards with higher values will tend to guess you have more money in your wallet, while people who see cards with lower values will tend to guess you have less money in your wallet. Kahneman and Tversky proved this concept of anchoring in a similar experiment involving spinning wheels and guesses about the composition of United Nations membership, which though it was more complicated to perform, did have the advantage of being a valid scientific study, unlike our little party trick.

There is another type of anchoring which is performed while being completely aware of the decision being made; this is the more commonly-known type of anchoring. George Akerlof confirmed this in his research on identity economics, although he never did explicitly say it was a form of anchoring. Instead, he noted that people will make economic decisions not just on their personal preferences, but based upon their social identity – that which is expected of them based on the social norms of the people they interact with. When talking about anchoring, the most common examples include social norms which evolved from the socioeconomic idiosyncrasies of the mid-20th century. We are, of course, talking about how everything should be based as a percentage of a person's income. For example, in many places around the world, it is common to say that an engagement ring should cost 2 months of your salary. There is no valid reason to believe this other than it has become a social norm of sorts, but it began in the 1980s when the diamond company DeBeers used a marketing campaign to convince people that this was the best way to show a potential marital partner your level of income and, thus, the quality of life they could expect. Other examples include expecting mortgage payments to be X percentage of your income, planning your investment portfolio based on some arbitrary retirement age that continuously increases, and so forth. This is one particular type of anchoring, which, for the sake of this book, we will call a "shallow anchor", because it is based entirely on social expectations. Social behavior most certainly shapes our behaviors, that is true, but this sort of behavior is much simpler in nature, and fully of the conscious mind. By contrast, what we will call a "deep anchor" occurs without a person being aware that the anchor has had an influence on their behavior, at all, such as with the experiments described using cards or spinners.

I, as your humble author, was not involved in any original research on anchoring, so I hope that those who were involved will excuse me for creating these labels of deep and shallow anchors. There is a clear and distinct difference, however. Each of these types of anchoring share the core trait in which a person's perception of the value of a thing is established, at least partially, by something completely irrelevant. That the anchor can be knowingly set as a result of social norms, or set unexpectedly as a result of guided expectation, means there are distinct methods by which that irrational perception of value is defined. So in lacking any existing terminology to differentiate between these unique anchors, it was necessary to invent terms in order to write this book.

At any rate, both types of anchoring have a significant impact on your investing behavior. It is much simpler to see shallow anchors. Today they are perpetuated primarily by people working as "financial advisers". Do not let the name fool you, as any schmuck can become a financial adviser, because it does not actually have anything to do with advising anyone – it is a sales job. The only prerequisite if you are selling certain types of financial products is that you must pass a brief multiple-choice test demonstrating that you know the laws that have been passed about those products. So, instead of actual financial advice, custom-tailored to the needs of the individual, what financial advisers generally offer is a standardized questionnaire you could easily answer on your own. You answer a few questions about your income, expenses, and age; and then the financial adviser provides you with a recommended anchor for your investment strategy. Usually it is in the form of "to retire at age 65 you should invest $X every month into this high-risk investment fund, and $Y every month into this low-risk investment fund, and over the years you should transfer more funds to the low-risk account as you get near retirement". Of course, you have to pay for every transaction you make, and their own pay is based on sales commissions of those transactions. The entire time, the real financial work is being done by quantitative analysts, researchers, risk managers, and so forth; none of it actually benefitting the individual investor. So, shallow anchoring during investing is a total and obvious bust that a lot of people manage to overcome relatively easily by either managing their investments themselves, or going to someone with real expertise that can teach them about their investments rather than simply trying to sell them something.

smbc-comics.com

Deep anchoring has a much more profound effect on investor behavior, though, and it is not so easy to even recognize it, much less overcome it. Simply put, your perception of the value of an investment is inherently shaped by thing you have experienced that day. Maybe the price of a stock dropped 10%, but you had a really good morning, so you have anchored the value of that stock to the previous price and estimate that it is just a temporary market undervaluation. It could be even more subtle than that. It has been demonstrated in several studies (it is a common one to replicate because it is easy to perform and kind of fun to watch) that when people hear a bit of bad news completely unrelated to investing, they will become more risk averse, perceiving investments to be more risky; whereas receiving a bit of good news will make people more prone to taking greater amounts of investment risk. Just like the Tversky and Kahneman's experiment with the wheel, a totally random event is guiding estimates of unrelated matters.

Unfortunately, as I am writing this book, there are no suggestions being made as to overcoming this form of anchoring. To borrow from cognitive-behavioral psychology, a clinical therapist might recommend spending a moment before you begin any period of investing decisions considering what you have done during the day so far, what you have seen and heard, and how it may have influenced your mood. In this way, it may help to prepare you to compensate for these influences, but as of yet there is no research to definitively demonstrate this is beneficial.

4.3 MENTAL ACCOUNTING

You may have heard someone say that they need to do some mental accounting, or even said the phrase yourself, when referring to the need to perform some basic financial calculations. Yeah, let us go ahead and ignore all that, because the fact of the matter is that this is rarely ever accounting in the true sense, nor is it performed mentally as often as people like to think (do not deny that you have used that calculator on your phone or put a pen to cocktail napkin before). Sure, that may be the casual use of the term "mental accounting", but for the sake of this book, we are going to be talking mental accounting in its true sense.

So, what is the formal usage of the term "mental accounting"? As you might have probably guessed, it does refer to actual accounting, in which a person is managing and recording the allocation of their financial assets. As for the "mental" element, I can only imagine that it is an insinuation that a person would have to be absolutely mental to manage their accounts in such a manner! What we are talking about is the tendency of people to separate their funds into different accounts under the belief that it is somehow beneficial, so there is nothing truly "mental" about this type of accounting, other than the reality that such behavior is merely a wacky construct of your mind rather than anything even resembling rationality. Perhaps a better name for mental accounting would be "partitioned accounting".

A common example of this type of behavior is keeping an "emergency fund". Maybe you keep a stash of cash buried in a bug-out-bag buried in the woods behind your house to ensure its readily available in case you need it in a hurry; more likely you have been told by someone that you should keep some cash in a savings account in case of unexpected medical bills or unemployment or something, despite the fact that the money is losing value as inflation causes prices to increase while your money sits around earning no interest. Maybe you have heard people talk about a financial windfall they have had lately – a tax return or a lucky bet at casino, and there is a good chance that since is money they have gained not included in their established accounting routine that they used that money to splurge, immediately squandering their improved financial state.

The closer you look at this thinking, the more obvious it becomes that a lot of it is total balderdash resulting our tendency to think about our money in different ways if we place labels on its usage or source, and none of it works to our own benefit. Sure, it is true that putting all your available money in a long-term retirement account will complicate things with the tax man, but what about all the money you are not saving for retirement? There are plenty of accounts that offer reasonable interest rates while keeping your money either freely available to you. As of writing this book, I am personally earning 3% annual interest on a checking account through a credit union, so what reason would I have for an emergency fund hidden away somewhere? You know that tax return you get every year? Why should it be seen differently than the rest of the income you earn every year, contributing to your overall financial success simply because it comes from a different source? What is the point if its value to you is gone nearly as quickly as it is realized?

In terms of equities, mental accounting takes the form of different investment portfolios. It is not uncommon for major investors to have a low-risk portfolio and a high-risk portfolio. Granted, if these investment portfolios are being managed by a fund manager, then it makes total sense to keep them separate so that the fund manager has options available for their customers. Unless that is your goal, though, separating these portfolios is a risk-management disaster just waiting to happen. By separating the two portfolios, you are actually distorting the total risk you are incurring, thereby resulting in a mismanagement of investments in each individual portfolio, compared to the reality that these portfolios are not separate – you own both of them regardless of how you keep track of them. In any case, you are doing nothing to benefit yourself than if you simply combined the two portfolios into a single large one.

Is it all hogwash, though? Of course there are ways to separate your investments that have legitimate functions. Retirement accounts are typically given special tax benefits, but should you try to use that money before reaching retirement age then there are also some pretty stiff penalties unless you are using it for one of a short list of very specific reasons. So, clearly, even if your retirement account has the best investment options, there are real financial reasons to avoid putting all your money in there.

Now comes a question which is likely to trigger some debate: Is investment diversification a form of mental accounting? The name Warren Buffett is likely familiar to you; famous investor, one of the richest people in the world, has something of a cult following. If not, it does not really matter, because all you really need to know is that his claim to success is something called "value investing". That means you find companies which are undervalued – they have a lot of success or value but the market price for their stocks is lower than you would expect. Buffett has been known to give the advice that you should put all your money into the best investments. After all, if you take some of your money and invest it in stocks are 2nd best, or 3rd best, or worse, then you are missing-out on the opportunity to earn more value, right? Of course, Even Buffett has invested in over 100 different companies, so maybe there really is something to the idea of diversification. If you put all your money in a single stock, and then that stock does poorly, then you lose everything. If you spread-out your investments across several stocks, and one of them does poorly, then there is a good chance that the others will remain stable or possibly even thrive. The idea behind diversification is to limit the amount of risk that you will lose value on the whole of your investment portfolio, and yet the more you diversify by investing in the stocks of less attractive companies, the more likely it becomes that one of the stocks in your portfolio will lose value. So, at what point does risk management become mental accounting, or is it all mental accounting applied in a questionably positive context?

4.4 NEPOTISM

This is a matter much simpler than any other discussed in this book, but no less profound. It is a matter so ubiquitous and obvious that most, if not every culture in history has had their own word for it. In China there is a term "guanxi" which refers to mutual interpersonal obligations which tend to take a central role even in matters of economics; the Arabic word "wasta" roughly refers to the amount of clout a person has to maintain preferential treatment; in English, the language in which this book has been written, we simply call it nepotism. Even in making our financial decisions, far too often it is about who you know, not what you know.

Take, for example, the career field of financial advisors. This is a commission-based sales job in which people try to get you to buy investments, or insurance, or annuities, or any of a variety of other financial products (the people who give actual financial advice are called Chartered Financial Analysts). The person needs to pass a short test to prove they know what the products are and that they know the laws related to the sales of those products, but they do not really need to know anything about finance. In fact, being well-versed in investing or finance is seen merely as a marketing ploy to attract customers and sell them pre-packaged financial products. It should come as no surprise, then, that rather than identifying and seeking-out a specific target customer, it is all about relationship sales. Generally it starts with family and friends, trying to use their relationship as leverage to obligate them into becoming customers. Then, acquaintances, maybe old coworkers, members of the same religious congregation or club, and so forth. Often you will find financial advisors represented at business networking events, and with every person they meet, they try to get referrals to meet other new people. Quite simply, it is the exact same approach used by certain makers of makeup, kitchenware, and dubious nutritional supplements. It is all sales-pitch, rather than legitimate financial analysis, but because there is some sort of social relationship involved, often people feel obligated to work with them. At the very least, being close to a person puts you in close proximity to their sales spiel frequently enough that you may eventually become convinced. No matter the case, this financial relationship is based on social engagement rather than competence.

These simple forms of nepotism shape investments in other ways, too. When a person is opening a business and needs start-up capital, often then people they will go to first are family and friends, either looking for loans or investors. Far too often, this results either in people investing in companies run by inexperienced individuals doomed to fail, or entrepreneurs getting suckered into unfavorable loan agreements.

Nepotism shapes the stock market in much more complex ways, though, too. The decisions that companies make in terms of choosing suppliers, the terms offered to customers, the regulations which dictate how a company can operate, and even the information shared between individuals are all far too frequently shaped by personal relationships. It may come as a surprise that elected officials are not subject to insider trading laws, creating a totally legal way for companies to bribe the government to pass favorable legislation. Collusion between investors and central banks to fix interest rates, or between investors and companies to artificially manipulate short-term financial performance metrics, or between investors and other investors to share information not yet available to the public (i.e.: insider trading) all creates inefficiencies within the investment markets for the sake of either mutual short-term gains, or personal obligation.

A few questions arise from this. How do you avoid participating in nepotism out of personal obligations? How can you identify nepotism in corporations in which you may have investment interest? How can you tell if there is some kind of collusion occurring in the market? Well, of the latter two problems, generally speaking there is not much you can do to identify it. Unless you take an extremely active role in the operations of the companies in which you invest, chances are you will not have access to the data you need to determine if there is nepotism occurring. You might try to identify specific cash flows then compare that to the market price during the time that a cash flow took place and see if something unusual happened, but your average investor simply will not have enough influence or regulatory authority to access detailed accounts which are more often than not considered proprietary information vital to staying competitive in the market. As for the first problem, all I can say is dig deep to find your assertive side and refuse. After all, if your money being put at risk, not theirs, so you are the one who is going to eventually come to regret a bad decision.

4.5 SATISFICING

Economists are fond of the idea that people, in acting rationally, will fully satisfy their wants and needs for the lowest possible cost. In fancy-talk, people will maximize their total utility or value. Maximized utility means the most benefit you can get, while maximized value means benefits divided by the cost of obtaining that benefit.

If you have ever spent any time trying to scrape money together for a bar crawl, you will know exactly what this is about. Let us say you shake $10 in change out of your couch cushions (immediately realizing that you need to clean your couch more frequently). To make the most of your night you want to determine how many beers and how many slices of pizza you can afford, and what combination of these two things will give you the most satisfaction for the night. Yeah, your standard Econ101 text will tell you that for each slice of pizza you eat, that the next slice will still increase your total satisfaction but not as much as the first one (called the law of diminishing marginal returns). What they do not tell you, though, is that for every beer you drink, your desire to measure any of this stuff quickly disappears, and you completely forget what you were doing in the first place. Let us step away from the Principles of Introductions example and look at something a little more relevant:

It has been shown in several studies that making voting mandatory does not actually have much influence on whether or not people participate, or whether those people will try to educate themselves on the facts. By contrast, making objective facts freely and easily available improves both voter participation and the degree to which voters are informed. This demonstrates that people are more engaged when they do not have to work as hard to become engaged.

We apply the same behaviors every single day of our lives. If you are at the store buying bourbon and Lucky Charms (breakfasts of champions!), there is a good chance that the store across the street is selling them at a lower price. Do you give a fuck? Well, maybe a little, but since you are not certain, you do not care enough to actually go find-out. You would have to go all the way across the street, spending time doing price comparisons, when you would rather just be at home getting hammered while watching The Price is Right. So, instead of ensuring that you are maximizing your utility, you decide to spend your money at the store you are already in.

Changing the example slightly, let us say the store you are currently in is out of the cheap bourbon, so the price of breakfast is really just too high for you. Now it is worth it for you to go across the street and see if they have the cheap stuff.

Suddenly, you have discovered your GAF: Give-a-Fuck Index.

Your GAF refers to your willingness to spend more time and energy to get better results. In the previous example, you can calculate your GAF very easily. Start by estimating the highest price you would be willing to pay before looking somewhere else, and then go find the cheapest price available in your area. If you would have paid \$15, but could have gotten it for \$10, then your GAF is $10/15 = 0.67$. In other words, yeah, you could have gotten a better price, but you did not give enough of a fuck to go find it; your GAF is less than 1, meaning you give less than 1 full fuck. If you give a fuck (1 full fuck), then you have surpassed the point in your GAF index that you are willing to go find a better price.

Sometimes this is a rational way to use your resources, such as deciding to hire someone to analyze your retirement investments. Sure, you could spend a lot of time teaching yourself econometrics and investing strategy and do the analysis yourself for free, but by the time you are ready, you have already lost a lot of money by keeping bad investments for so many years. In this case, your GAF is decided for you, in that the cost of hiring someone must be less than the benefits spending time to learn how to do it yourself in order to keep your GAF below 1.

By the way, there are terms for this stuff. The idea that people maximize the benefits of their decisions is called "satisfying", and the idea that people will make the best decision possible given limited information or limited motivation is called "satisficing". Think of satisficing as the actions of "good enough".

Investor A

Is borrowing a total of $1 million to invest in mutual funds, and has 10 different lenders willing to lend that money. Investor A studies each of them carefully, comparing the interest rates that each charges in the hopes of getting the lowest costs for his investment. During this research, it is revealed that for every additional $1 thousand in loans requested from a single lender, that the lender increases the interest rate. So, even though a single lender might charge the lowest interest rates on the first $1 thousand, if too much money is borrowed from that lender, it will start charging interest rates higher than its competitors. So, Investor A carefully calculates how much money to borrow from each lender in order to get the lowest total cost. That investor then carefully studies the different mutual funds available, calculating the potential risk and returns of each, and deciding how to allocate their investment funds based on their goals.

Investor B

Is also borrowing a total of $1 million to invest in mutual funds, calls around to the first 10 lenders they can find through an internet search, and borrows all of it from the one with the lowest stated interest rate. They then turn on CNBC and invest all their money in the mutual fund that sounds best by some person who sounds like they know what they are talking about.

Clearly there is a difference in behaviors, there. Investor A is behaving in a way that satisfies – they are maximizing the total benefits of their financial activity in a rational way. Investor B is not too worried about it, and makes the most of their decision while putting forth as much effort as they care to.

The behaviors of Investor B are known as satisficing, which is a portmanteau. Sort of like the way "edutainment" is a combination of "education" and "entertainment", "satisficing" combines "satisfying" and "sufficing". Satisficing is the behavior of "good enough". Could you more effectively manage your money? Yeah, but so what? Regardless of whether this is a responsible approach to financial management, it is an extremely common one, and one with implications worth measuring.

The focus of satisficing studies tend to focus primarily on labor productivity and managerial decisions. Of the former, there has been interest in the matter of people failing to properly perform their jobs to the best of their ability, result-ing in increased workloads for their colleagues (an issue technically known as "freeriding"), or else resulting simply in less work being performed and perhaps at a lower quality. There is a wealth of research on this matter in the study of motivational theory, but that is outside the scope of this book. Of the latter, there is great concern regarding the matter of bounded rationality, which refers to the necessity of people to make decisions despite being less than fully informed of those matter relevant to the decision. Herbert Simon would likely be thrilled to know that up until this very moment you gave no consideration to the fact that he first identified satisficing behavior in the 1940s or 1950s, because it proves his theory that you were able to acquire information about satisficing from this book that was good enough to meet your minimum expectations without know-ing all the details. That was the original point, after all: The whole concept was studied as a way to show that people make decisions when there is not enough information available to identify the optimal solution. Simon was able to prove that in any risky decision, a person will not have all the information needed to be completely certain they are making the best choice available. Rather, since ignorance is an inherent part of every decision we make, we look not to optimize our decisions but to find the decision which meets the minimum requirements necessary to be considered acceptable.

It might have occurred to you by this point that satisficing behavior has something of a perceptual duality to it. There are contexts in which satisfic-ing behavior is studied within the context of some preventable deficiency, and legitimately so, but it must also be recognized that bounded rationality is real-ity: it is quite impossible, much less efficient in terms of cost and time, for any person to have literally all the information needed to guarantee an optimal out-come. When it comes to investing, both apply. There is never a time when we can fully have all the information we could possibly need to know the outcome of an investment, and that uncertainty is what we call risk. We try our best to limit the amount of uncertainty by identifying variables which influence the out-comes of investments and incorporating them into ever-more complex models and algorithms, succeeding so very slowly in eliminating that uncertainty bit by bit, yet it will remain for the foreseeable future, and so we seek to manage it. We take whole piles of investments and use statistical methods such as "value at risk" or "expected shortfall" to try and manage how much value is can be lost under the worst (for example) 5% probability of cases, or to estimate what the maximum losses will be under the worst case scenario. The point is that when we absolutely cannot have all the information we need to make optimal decisions, we try to convince ourselves of certainty by making complex calcu-lations of how much we are uncertain. These methods can be very useful, that is true, but the longer it has been since experiencing a significant loss, the GAF index slowly drops and the other types of satisficing take-over. This seems to be common among institutional investors; lenders will issue higher-risk loans in search of higher profits without more thoroughly exploring why each case was considered higher-risk; or stock investors will become complacent and buy or sell stocks based purely on observed movement without asking why those movements are occurring (see Chapter 5.6). Among non-investors, there is a tendency for a person who has better information available to simply be intimidated by the idea of stock investing, or else they turn to their brother-in-law who just got his series 7 license as a financial adviser (see the portion of this chapter on nepotism). Then there are those situation where there are influences on you to act fast, and although there is information readily available, the anxiety you feel drives-down your GAF index and you invest anyway just so that you do not miss an opportunity (see Chapter 6.1).

As already noted, there are statistical tools available for you to minimize the impact of satisficing behavior on your investment portfolio, but unfortunately there are not many good ways to prevent yourself from satisficing in the first place. The reason for that is simple: it is impossible to fully satisfy the needs of an investment decision – there will always be uncertainty – and even if it was possible there is still the matter of prudency. A decision must be made, and if you give too much of a fuck about it, then you may just end-up subjecting yourself to "analysis paralysis". So, the real key is to find a proper balance – you must care enough to be responsible with your investment decisions, but not care so much that you give yourself panic attacks at the very thought of investing. Also, it does not hurt to pre-program the analyses you use to make your decisions so a computer can do it more quickly than you can.

4.6 RATIONAL IGNORANCE

For investors it is especially profound to understand the nature of satisficing because they make ignorant choices every day and have sought ways to improve the quality of the decisions without actually becoming more informed. In fairness, if we knew everything there was to know, then there would be no risk to investing, so financial risk is inherently defined as the degree of uncertainty for potential losses in value. Even if we knew for certain about a particular loss, then it would still just be considered a cost, rather than some uncertainty that a cost might be incurred. Investors know they will never eliminate their own ignorance, so to compensate for this they have spent massive volumes of time and money developing tools and strategies that mitigate the negative impact of that ignorance. Since risk inherently stems from uncertainty, and uncertainty is measured and calculated using statistics, the tools that have been developed to manage risk are all based on statistical analysis; or the probability-weighted distribution of risk among groups of people taking the same risk (see the section of this chapter on satisficing).

Rational ignorance refers to the state in which it actually makes more sense to remain uncertain. It is a coin termed by Anthony Downs and was originally applied regarding politics and the cost of acquiring information and voter participation. This results when there are costs higher than the value of obtaining the information. For a certain class of investors, this typically means lost time. Obscene amounts of money have been spent increasing the speed with which investment transactions can be made. For example, in 2011, a fiberoptic cable was installed at the bottom of the Atlantic Ocean at a cost of $300 million, just so that financial transactions exclusively between New York and London could be 5 milliseconds faster. That is the time it takes for a honey bee to flap its wings just once. So, as you can imagine, people are extremely serious when they say "time is money". What they mean, though, is that by delaying a transaction even slightly, they are missing an opportunity, so if they took the time to worry about performing a proper analysis, or even fact-checking something, then it would cost them money in lost opportunity – something economists call "opportunity cost". Of course, as discussed in Chapter 4.5, ignorance is risk, and traders are so insistent that time has so much value that it is worth the risk to go as far as to automate their trades by algorithm, so it does not even matter what is being bought or sold, so long as the price is right.

It is also a phenomenon that when people spend a lot of money or put a lot of effort into something, even if it was a bad decision, they will try to justify it to themselves by convincing themselves the decision they made had greater value than it really did (this is related to the Gambler's Fallacy, discussed in Chapter 6.2). So, it is generally a bad idea to point-out that unmanaged index funds which do not require people to make decisions systematically thwomp managed funds in which someone actively decides how to invest the fund's money, by generating higher returns. Fund managers do not like to hear that, though whether or not they are aware of it, there is a little trick they use to match the returns on index funds discussed in Chapter 6.4.

CONCLUSION

So as you can see, in the end, you may not even be aware that your personal behaviors are harming your finances, or maybe you are aware of it and your GAF index is simply too low to do anything about it, or maybe you care but feel obligated to do what is proper. No matter, eventually our bad behaviors always catch-up with us, and unless you take steps to be proactive in preventing these behaviors, you will only notice them in hindsight, coming to regret a lifetime of living on the edge.

Chapter 5

Problematic Perception

What you see around you is not reality. The experiences you have of your daily life do not actually exist as you know them. They are merely constructs of your mind – interpretations of sensory information to which you are exposed that is then translated into something comprehensible only within the context of what you think you already know. Even the raw, measured data to which we are exposed is taken for granted as an objective, undeniable fact; yet even within this our own minds deceive us. The only fact is that nothing is true, and we must peer deeper within ourselves and within others, embracing the madness inherent in us all, so that we might function within the chaos we create rather than build illusory structures of reality which are doomed to fade into the ethereal void of our mind's perception.

Ok, it was fun being Guru Mike for a bit, and everything in the preceding paragraph is true, in its own way, but let us talk about this in terms that do not reek of new-age cultists. The problems surrounding perception (in an otherwise healthy individual) comes primarily from the frontal lobe. Yes, as the name suggests, that the part of your brain that is in the front of your, right behind that whole facial-region on your head. This is the part of the brain that allows you to make sense of the world. It all starts when your senses (sight, sound, etc.) are stimulated by something around you. Maybe it is the droning sound of some schmuck giving a PowerPoint presentation on the tax implications of changing how your company treats asset deprecation, or the sharp pain of an elbow to your side as the person next to you wakes you so the boss does not see you drooling on the brand new conference table. Either way, all that information is turned into electrochemical signals in your nervous system which is then sent to the parietal lobe of the brain to determine what type of information it is and how to process it. Whether it is purely sensory information being processed, or whether that sensory information contains encoded data such as stock performance data, it all gets sorted-out in the parietal lobe, and then sent to the frontal lobe where it is processed in a way that you can consciously understand. Even better, in the frontal lobe, you can do something process something called "inductive logic". This is the process by which you take information you know and use it to find patterns and discover abstract principles, allowing you to make predictions about the outcomes of events, your actions and, most importantly to this chapter, how the information you have received fits within the context of what you already know. With all these steps required for your brain to understand the world around you, there is plenty that goes wrong every single time, and that is where things become problematic.

5.1 INFORMATION ASYMMETRY

In a world where capital markets are dominated by the forces of good and evil, the fate of humanity lies in the hands of a single force. It is a power greater than any individual can hope to possibly wield, and has the power to destroy those who try, yet it remains our only hope. That force is called Information Asymmetry!

Really, though, information asymmetry is both a fundamental principle of modern economics which allows our society of function and grow, yet at the same time it has the potential to be used for manipulative reasons. Since the topic made it into this book, you probably do not need much help guessing which aspect of information asymmetry is more prevalent among equities markets.

It goes without saying that not everyone knows all the same stuff. In fact, it is unlikely that any two people have identical sets of information stored in their brains. This has actually been extremely useful, because otherwise modern civilization would not exist, at all. One of the most basic principles of economics is that specialization of knowledge and the division of labor is a primary source of modern societies. What this means is that you get good at a particular type of work, let us say you are a farmer, and you can perform it very quickly and efficiently without trouble. Someone else does the same thing, but with a different job, in the case they are good at making tools. Well, rather than each of you wasting time and resources doing the things you are bad at, you instead produce more of the things you are good at and then trade. You give them food, and they give you tools. Sure, you could make your own tools, but you suck at it so you would spend the whole day getting almost nothing done. Instead, go with what you know, so that together you can produce more total stuff than you could if you did not work together. That is called "gains from trade". Of course, reality is a little more complicated, given the huge number of people with a vast range of skills, and money was developed as a way to ensure you get something of value for your work even if the other person does not have anything to barter that you want. Despite the complexity that comes with sheer size, the entire system relies on the basic principles of specialization, division of labor, and gain from trade. Even in the stock market, researchers and quantitative analysts like myself have a very specialized skill set, and we provide that to investors of all types (generally funds and brokerage firms, since they are the only ones who can afford to hire us full-time) so that they can use that information to help guide their decisions. In exchange, we get paid and use that money to buy produce, since all the food I try to grow on my own seems to die.

That is all the good side of asymmetric information. There is a more troublesome side to it, though, as thoroughly explored by George Akerlof. Information has value, and if someone has information you need to make a decision, frequently they will not be so ready to give it away freely. For example, in the US,

financial advisers are legally allowed to lie directly to your face and make recommendations or take other actions that screw you financially. This is common
practice in the industry, because financial advisers are paid a commission for
every transaction their clients make. Under President Obama they passed a rule
that would prevent this practice called "the fiduciary rule", but his successor to
the presidency is intent on ensuring that the rule never takes effect. This particular example exhibits a specific type of information asymmetry called "adverse
selection". Simply put, one party to a transaction has more information than
the other, and that difference in information is abused to gain an advantage in
negotiations. This is also common among "Wall Street insiders" – people who
work directly in the investment markets and use their position to either acquire
or spread information that is not otherwise available to the public. In some cases
this would be considered illegal, and in others it is not, but even the illegal transactions that take place are completely legal for federal elected officials in the US,
allowing them to trade on confidential government information, or information
from industry insiders in exchange for favors. In 2012, the STOCK ACT was
passed, designed to bring an end to this practice, but many loopholes remained,
and important parts of the act were removed to largely make the act ineffective.

A second specific type of negative information asymmetry is called "moral
hazard". This occurs not during a transaction, but when one person is acting on
behalf of another. The information asymmetry occurs when the person functioning as a representative knows more about their full intentions and future actions
than the person being represented. For example, you may trust a fund manager
to make reasonable investments with low risk, but that manager actually takes
much greater risks than promised. Such behaviors are widely cited as a contributing factor to the subprime mortgage crisis, in which lenders were issuing
tremendously high loans then hiding the amount of risk in investments that bun-
dled large volumes of loans together, so that their investors were not aware of
how much risk was really being incurred and distributed.

The negative effects of information asymmetry are simple to understand:
You are not privileged enough to have the most up-to-date information, leaving your investments perpetually underperforming compared to their potential
if you were trading under optimal conditions; and you are highly likely to get
ripped-off by someone who knows more than you.

You can protect yourself, though. First, remember that the financial sector
as a whole, and especially the investments industry, is really shady – filled with
con-artists and scum bags. Navigating the world of investing looking for good
investments is like swimming in shark-infested waters looking for a steak. Oddly
enough, it does not seem to cross anyone's mind that if lenders and managers
stopped taking excessive risks, and that if everyone actually worked in the best
interest of their clients, that they would actually have an advantage, attracting
more customers because they know that person can be trusted. So, this is a behavior which screws not just you, but the stock markets as a whole. So, anytime
you are dealing with investments, always go into any meeting or transaction

telling yourself over and over: "No one cares about my finances as much as I do." It is your money, you decide what to do with it, so do not let anyone convince you to do something that is not in your best interest, or which seems shady.

Other methods to protect yourself from information asymmetry is to educate yourself. Make sure you learn about investing, investigate your investment options yourself, and know exactly what you want to do before attempting to contact anyone. If you do not have the time or inclination to learn a whole new skill set, or if you are considering taking the advice something else gives you, then get a second opinion first. See what other people in the industry say by directly asking other people in the industry. Do not be afraid to shop-around before committing, and if you have few bucks to spare you might consider hiring a finance professor or analyst as a consult to evaluate the recommendations being made. Since these people do not have anything to gain or lose based on your decision, you are far more likely to get an unbiased, well-informed recommendation.

5.2 ENDOWMENT EFFECT

There is something you need to know. The stuff I own is more valuable than the stuff you own. Even if you own something that is identical in every way to the thing I own, mine is worth more simply because I own it instead of you. No, I am not being a total jerk. Ok, well, yes, I am being a total jerk, but so are you, and so is everyone else living on planet earth. This is a phenomenon imbedded so deeply within us, that it is not even unique to humans, either – other primates exhibit this behavior, too. The endowment effect is a simple concept that exists universally, yet no one has been able to figure-out exactly what causes it or why.

The endowment effect merely means that people place greater value on things they already own than things they do not own. In an experiment that has been replicated by a number of researchers arguing over the validity of the conclusions being drawn, people are given items of equal value (originally some people were given a chocolate bar and others a coffee mug). Regardless of which item a person received, participants in these studies were resistant to the idea of trading for the other item. Clearly chocolates and mugs are very different things, and people will have their own preference for each, creating problems in the initial research on the endowment effect, but a large volume of studies came to follow which better confirmed its existence, and even developed a model to measure it. The whole thing is mathematically measured using WTAP models, which refers to the differential analysis between "willingness to accept" and "willingness to pay". In a 2000 study by Carmon and Ariely, it was found that people's willingness to accept money in exchange for tickets to high profile sporting events were 14 times greater than their willingness to pay for those same tickets, demonstrating a clear, measurable difference in the perceived value of those tickets. This WTAP differential has been used to measure the endowment effects in a wide range of studies using a variety of populations of both people and animals, and a variety of goods. The only matter of debate is the cause.

The majority of theories behind why this occurs relies on the principles of prospect theory (discussed in Chapter 5.2). Simply put, these theories state that people are more averse to loss than they are attracted to gain, so giving away something of ownership is considered a loss and will be weighed more heavily than the value they gain in exchange. Related to this is a somewhat different theory – that of "a bird in the hand is worth two in the bush". In other words, if a person already has something of value, then there is no reason for them to incur the risk of a regrettable exchange for something of equivalent value. The uncertainty of the exchange being proposed inherently comes with a degree of risk, no matter how small, and so it is not a person's aversion to loss, but their aversion to risk, which makes them demand a price premium for the things they own. This theory (which, to my knowledge, was first developed by me) fits the existing research more effectively than loss aversion models, in that the research on the endowment effect universally puts people in a situation of considering the scarcity of the item they are holding. If something is more scarce, such as tickets to high profile sporting events, then the amount of risk they incur by giving them away is much higher because the odds of them being able to buy another set of tickets is extremely low. By contrast, in 1994, Shogrun et al. performed an experiment in which the perception of scarcity was minimal, resulting in data demonstrating that the WTAP differential was nearly non-existent. Yet another theory is simply that people make attachments to the things they own, whether emotional attachments or incorporating the item into their own sense of identity as expressed through their own asset value, making it more difficult for them to let go of the items in their possession. Yet another theory states that we have evolved to favor those things we already own as an inherent instinct to improve our negotiating decision during bartering. While some of these explanations seems to make more sense than others, I personally favor the theory which explains WTAP differentials in terms of risk premiums, and not just because it is the most convenient explanation for its role in stock markets (although that does seem to provide some circumstantial evidence to support the idea). Still, the theories which involve loss aversion seem to be most robustly supported by prospect theory and the disposition effect, both of which are discussed later in this chapter.

At any rate, investing markets. Endowment effect. People acting dumb. These things go together like gin and tonic water... and a lime wedge... maybe with just a bit of elderflower liqueur. It is a heady tonic that swirls together in glistening beauty as you stir with ice, each ingredient dancing with the others yet somehow remaining separate just long enough to provide us with a visual representation of chaotic beauty. Wait, was that a metaphor for how people behave on the stock market? I suppose you have a group of separate people all with their distinct notes to contribute to the value of an asset, each remaining separate for as long as possible due to differences in the perception of value, but as they all twirl around each other finding a proper match for negotiations, finally the ingredients merge into a moderate compromise. Then again, maybe it is just happy hour at the local bar.

In any case, the endowment effect is largely to blame for failed investment transactions. Not bad investments, mind you, but transactions which never actually occur. Those willing to sell and those willing to buy do not agree upon a price due to differences in the perception of the value of the assets being proposed for exchange. Something this is beneficial, as it is a poor investor who will buy at high prices and sell for low prices, yet at the same time we must be aware that this does not become extreme to the degree that it is problematic. One may find themselves holding onto an asset with unrealistic expectations of its true value, only to discover that the market price will never reach that high, at which point they may have to settle for an even lower price than was previously available. A person waiting for a stock price to drop below a certain level before buying may never get that opportunity, and miss the opportunity of a lifetime. This would be particularly dangerous if you are short-selling (i.e.: selling a stock with the contractual agreement that you will buy it back at a later date). In such a case, so long as the price of the stock keeps going up, you have everything in the world to lose, because you eventually have to rebuy that stock and there is no upper limit on stock prices – only lower limits, which is $0 (unless you are buying on margin, which is a type of investment loan, in which case you would need to repay the interest cost of the loan).

To make a long story short, the endowment effect is within each of us. Our perceptions of value are all messed-up based purely on ownership, and that can make for sub-optimal investing decisions. So, what can you do to prevent the endowment effect from influencing your decisions? Not much, honestly, but it can be helpful to remind yourself that there are plenty of options available – not only are there ample volumes of stocks, but you do not have to choose to do anything right away. The studies showed that reducing the perception of scarcity helped to mitigate the effects of the endowment effect, so by keeping an eye on several different investment options rather than just a single stock, or remembering that you can always try again tomorrow, it should help take some of the pressure off your desire to irrationally covet your own assets like some lunatic obsessed with a precious ring.

5.3 PROSPECT THEORY

When it comes to modern portfolio theory (which is the formal name given to basically any analysis of the relationship between investing risk and reward), everyone's brain just seems to shut-down. Somewhere along the way, very legitimate and rational behaviors turned into a mantra of "more risk = more reward". It is as if the very nature of taking huge risks inherently meant a person was guaranteed to earn more money on their investments rather than lose everything because they put all their money into bad investments like a dummy. Of course, like everything we talk about in this book, the cause of this phenomenon is hard-wired into our brains – we are each prone to making this mistake and must be careful to check ourselves.

The discovery of prospect theory by Kahneman and Tversky in the 1970s was one of the most quintessentially defining moments of behavioral economics. It was a huge discovery, it expanded into a lot of other discoveries using research based upon the same methods, and it is been confirmed to have a neurological basis by using brain scans. So, this is one of those undeniable principles which originally gave behavioral economics a reputation of validity within the greater economics community. This is when the world really dropped the assumption that people make rational decisions, and started to listen when behavioral researchers were saying that our economic decisions were completely insane.

Prospect theory is named as a result of people being presented with several prospective choices, and much choose one. Every action we take, or do not take, is the result of our assessment of the available options and the picking one of them to pursue. When it comes to decisions of value and risk, however, the manner in which we make our decisions gets a bit quirky. They dynamic duo who developed prospect theory identified it as having 2 distinct elements, both of which contributed to irrational decision-making. The first they called the certainty effect, which is a phenomenon in which people are risk averse when a guaranteed gain is possible, even if a much better option is likely but not guaranteed. By contrast, the certainty effect also includes the tendency of people to increase risk-taking behaviors, trying to avoid a certain loss, even if the alternative option poses the threat of a greater loss but it is not certain.

The second element of prospect theory is called the isolation effect, which states that when people are presented with multiple choices, they will try to simplify their choice through the process of elimination. People will completely ignore any elements that all the choices share, then compare the things which are different. While this seems reasonable at first, it leads to inconsistencies when the same decision is presented in different ways.

The results of these two elements is that people stop looking at actual likelihood and value of the final outcome of their decisions, and instead look at the potential for gains and losses. It was noted that people consistently underestimate the probabilities of something happening, and especially so when it comes to potential losses. As a result, people will go for the sure thing, even if it is the worse outcome. A strange contrast occurred, however, at the extremes of probability, at which point people strongly overestimated the odds of a particular outcome. The popularity of gambling and insurance is attributed to this perceptual shift in the likelihood of an event occurring.

In other words, people dismiss things which are likely to occur if there is an option with certainty, but when things are highly unlikely to occur then suddenly people start making their decisions based on the extremes. In investing, there is never a shortage of extreme risks which people can pursue, and far too often they are happy to try. There is a glorification of this in investor culture – a noble pursuit of the impossible only to return with untold riches. This is the realm of speculative investing, which refers to investing in stocks of companies that are very small, very new, whose operations are uncertain, and so forth. For example, small medical research firms and start-up tech companies are typically considered very speculative because they're not proven to be well-managed, and oftentimes the success of the company depends on their research yielding positive results of a discovery. If they succeed, then these companies are frequently bought by much larger companies and the cheapo stock you bought in a high-risk company skyrockets in value as the larger company purchases all, or a controlling share of the stock, driving up its market price. Even the most conservative of investment portfolios tends to have at least a small percentage of its value dedicated to speculative investments.

So, why invest in stocks at all, though? Why not invest in treasury bills (a type of short-term government debt), which are considered "risk free" – a guaranteed thing. Quite simply, it is because the guarantee with treasury bills is that they have rates of return lower than average inflation rates, which means that the longer an investor holds onto risk free investments, their investments will lose value in the sense that they will not be able to purchase as much. If a treasury bill is paying 1% annual interest (and they are never that high), but inflation is 2%, then the cost to buy things is increasing faster than the money you are earning. So, the guarantee is not one of a gain that would attract investors away from something much greater but uncertain; the guarantee is one of loss that makes people search for riskier alternatives to avoid loss. Somewhere along the way, this all became really exaggerated so that people now actually believe that they should be looking for risk to earn rewards, rather than demanding higher rewards from higher-risk investments.

Since the decision-making process described by prospect theory inherently leads us to make irrational investment choices, we must learn a new decision-making process. That's where modern portfolio theory comes into play. There's good news and bad news to that. The bad news is that you will have to learn some basic statistics in order to incorporate any of it into your investment decisions. Sorry, it is unavoidable. The good news is that once you have learned the basics, you can easily customize your own valuation models which estimate the likelihood of events occurring and adjusting the estimated value of each decision by the probability of it occurring. Unfortunately, as we discussed earlier in Chapter 5.1, and will touch-on again later in this chapter, your estimates will still be wrong, but at the very least they'll be based on calculated and thoughtful logic, rather than bizarre interpretations of the information being presented to you, dependent more on the presentation of that information than the content.

5.4 DISPOSITION EFFECT

There are many investing strategies which involve selling stocks after the market price has exceeded a specific price – a calculated decision that a company's stock has a maximum value and that if the market price goes higher than that, it must eventually come down again, and so they sell that stock to avoid the risk. In the same line of strategy, an investor might see that there is a company with value, and that if the market price of their stock drops below some minimum milestone, then they will buy it. In fact, some of the most common types of transactions called a "limit order", in which an investor tells their broker to buy a stock if its price drops below the lower limit, or to sell a stock if its price rises above the upper limit. Other strategies which have gained popularity over the past couple of decades involve something called "countercyclical investing", in which a person gradually sells shares as their market prices increase, and buy shares as market prices decrease. After all, is not it the entire point of investing to buy shares cheaply and sell them at a price premium? (Note: Countercyclical investing should not be confused with a countercyclical stock, which is a stock whose value tends to move in opposite directions of the rest of the market.)

These types of common investing strategies stem from a behavioral anomaly known as the disposition effect. The examples given so far seem so rational, though, do not they? To get a better sense of how the disposition effect can make us act nutty, let us use the classic example of investors studied by Terrance Odean back in the 1990s. Odean looked at the investing behavior of 10,000 accounts (which is an admirably-large sample size, so much so that it might, itself, qualify for a chapter in this book of mad behavior), and did some calculations to measure how quickly investors responded to changes in the price of a stock. What he found was that when people made money, they were very quick to sell that stock as soon as possible; they wanted to "stop while they are ahead". By contrast, people who lost money on a stock that was losing value kept holding that stock for far longer than they should have, experiencing greater losses than necessary while hoping so hard that the price of their stocks will go back up again.

In other words, traders are so mental that they are doing exactly the opposite of what makes any kind of sense – failing to act while losing money, and pulling-out of the market once they start to earn a profit. To make things worse is that this kind of absurdity is so common that it has become a standard institution of specific types of buy and sell orders, and investing strategies. Investors will use equations and models and try to validate the idea. It is, after all, the entire basis of stock trading to take advantage of movement in the markets. In theory, it is completely rational to buy and sell stocks when they either approach or exceed upper or lower limits in price. In practice, however, people are not very good at estimating what the upper and lower limits should be, nor do they have much reason to believe that a stock's market price will shift direction at any given point, resulting in the systematic perpetuation of an epic failure of an otherwise good idea. In the end, what looks at first to be important and rational methods of managing investments, when put into practice almost immediately fails. Since these approaches to investing have become such a pillar of finance, what we really get is a sort-of mass hysteria.

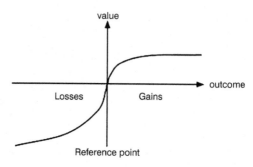

FIGURE 5.1   Loss Aversion

The cause, at its root, it that we are emotionally reactionary creatures, prone to violating our own strategies, or even going as far as to incorporate our neurosis directly into automated strategies. More specifically, the cause is tied to prospect theory (discussed in Chapter 5.3). The originators of the research behind the disposition effect, Shefrin and Statman (1985), noted that, "people dislike incurring losses much more than they enjoy making gains", which is consistent with the observations behind prospect theory in that people respond more strongly to potential losses than they respond to potential gains. This relationship also explains the Gamber's Fallacy (discussed in Chapter 6.2), wherein people want desperately to regain their losses despite no evidence that it is possible, resulting in further losses. This has been generically modeled as shown in Fig. 5.1.

To avoid the disposition effect is difficult, but possible. Albert Phung, for the website Investopia, writes that investors can use something he coins "hedonic framing". Simply put, rather than looking at large wins or large losses that could occur, or already have, look at them in terms of a series of smaller wins or losses. According to Phung, this can help investors to look at the situation and limit the emotional response to losses by thinking of them in smaller increments, and continue to incur wins by looking for the next. While I respect Phung, this sounds like dangerous nonsense. By breaking-up the total value of wins and losses into smaller increments, you are actually perpetuating the disposition effect, making it worse. In a position of losing money an investor will rationalize to themselves that they do not need to regain their total losses, only some smaller increment of it. In a position of gaining money, thinking about their gain in terms of smaller increments will function as a catalyst for the investor to pursue gain beyond what is reasonable. Eventually the maximum gains possible becomes the reference point for the investor, and the investor seeks to regain those losses from the peak, due to thinking of investments exclusively in terms of small increments.

Instead, to avoid the disposition effect, do not focus on gain or losses at all, and focus on value. There are two ways this can occur. The first is the preaching of the value investor – those people who dogmatically praise the long-term investments in companies that they see as undervalued given their long-run growth potential. Just because value investors tend to be a bit evangelical in their worship at the altar of Warren Buffett does not mean they are wrong. The stock market jumps around like Tigger on cocaine in the short-run, but there are long-term trends which can be identified and taken advantage of, but only if you have some estimate of what the true value of a company is, buy the stock while its undervalued, then hold it at least until it reaches that estimated value, if not longer (especially if the estimated value increases during that time). It can be difficult, but ignoring the daily madness of the market is beneficial for the vast majority. The second way to focus on value is more used more commonly by traders than value investors, but can be a useful tool for anyone. What we are talking about is looking at stress. This is best accomplished if you have a bit of statistical know-how, but can be done by just about anyone who can calculate simple averages. Looking at the volatility of a stock, its highest or lowest prices on the market can be estimated by tracking the changes in positive and negative movements in price. If a stock is performing well, but its average increases in price start to slow-down and the average decreases in price start to gain momentum, it may be a good idea to pull-out, at least until you can determine whether it is a temporary situation. By contrast, if a stock is losing value, sell it and if you really think it is going to rebound, then you might want to consider waiting until average increases in market price start to gain momentum over average decreases in market price. For all the movement in market price that a single stock will experience over the course of a single hour, knowing when to recognize a trend can be difficult, and it is all based on time-frame. You will most likely get very different estimates of when to buy and sell if you are averaging changes in the direction of volatility over the course of 1 hour than you will averaging those same changes over the course of 1 week, or 1 month. Unfortunately there is no universally correct answer to that, but at the very least you are thinking more rationally than you would be if you were stuck in the grip of the disposition effect.

5.5   ILLUSORY CONTROL

The environment in which equity traders work maintains the ideal conditions to foster delusions – ideas or beliefs which are starkly contradictory to reality, resulting from mental illness. Yup, you read that right: The trading environment takes people who are otherwise normal, mentally healthy individuals, and twists their minds to develop delusions that have clear and measurable negative consequences on the life of that individual. Given that mental illness is defined and diagnosed largely on whether a person's mental state has negative consequences on their life, and that the delusions which are created within the trading environment do cause very specific negative consequences, it can be said that working in the stock market will drive a person to madness. Chapter 7 will delve into the matter of psychological problems related to stress, but even more bizarre is the phenomenon in which people working as stock traders develop the delusion of illusory control. It is a sort-of god-like complex in which a person comes to believe they can control things over which they have absolutely no influence.

The first to definitively demonstrate that such delusions exist in a clinical setting was Langer in 1975. During the same study, he also demonstrated two of the most influential environmental factors that contributes to increasing a person's chance for developing these delusions. The first is competitiveness: A competitive environment increases the probability that a person will develop delusions of illusory control. The second identified by Langer is that of involvement and choice. To foster the delusion of control, a person must be actively involved in the environment, since a passive observer would inherently not be attempting to exert control and therefore could not develop a false sense of control. Particularly influential is when the person who is actively participating in the environment has the responsibility of making choices. The involvement of choice requires an individual to rely on "skill cues", in which a person's decisions appear to be based on their understanding of particular cues, such as market and stock metrics, and that their performance is measured either confirming or denying the degree of skill demonstrated within the environment. It is a tantalizing thought, that an individual can control their own performance on the stock market just by making the best decisions, but it is utter nonsense, as we will discuss shortly.

Since Langer, others have identified additional factors which contribute to the development of illusory control in individuals. In 1989, Gollwitzer and Kinney did a study demonstrating that illusory control is much more common and much more severe in an environment which requires one to adopt what they call an "implemental mindset". In normal-people speak, that means illusory control is more common in a goal-oriented environment in which a person is required to reflect upon their performance. Whether or not a person's actions have led to specific performance milestones forces that person to evaluate the consequences on their decisions and place the onus of control on themselves for the outcome. Particularly in the world of trading, where investors and fund managers are carefully evaluated, and their pay is based upon that performance, this has a particularly strong influence on people since it is being reinforced through operant conditioning (punishments and rewards). This begins immediately in the career of traders, because even if they do not yet have confidence in themselves, they need to portray both confidence and competence to potential customers in order to entice those potential customers and gain their trust. By exhibiting these behaviors of confidence beyond reality it creates something in the brain called a feedback loop, which is basically the "fake it till you make it" concept. By acting and speaking confidently on a regular, they are tricking their own brains into becoming convinced that it is a reality. This is a common clinical practice for patients with depression, wherein they will regularly focus on positive things and try to repress negative thoughts to break the cycle of negativity. By thinking about good things you feel better, and when you feel better you think more about good things, creating a cyclical feedback loop that can help some patients with depression. Well, this same process, when applied to confidence, may be the first harbinger of bad things to come for investors.

Later, in 1992, Friedland et al. demonstrated that a high-stress environment also strongly contributed to the development of illusory control within individuals. Stress is discussed in more detail in Chapter 7, but for the time being it should suffice to say that equity traders function is an extremely high-stress environment that inherently requires people to function with a great degree of uncertainty and make decisions at a rapid rate, and with consequences of great significance not only to their own careers but to the savings of a vast number of people. In fact, this was proven by Kahn and Cooper in 1993 who proved that traders have a significantly higher levels of "free-floating anxiety" as compared to the general population. According to Kahn and Cooper, a large contributor to the elevated levels of stress was the highly competitive environment in which traders function, which you will recognize has being one of the first factors identified as contributing to illusory control. So, not only do traders function in an environment rampant with 4 major causes of these delusions, but each of these factors contributes to the others, magnifying their intensity on the individual. Most people do not stand a chance of preventing these delusions entirely.

Mental quirks like delusions are not always indicative of mental illness, though. The measure of that is whether or not the quirk has a negative impact on your life. Well, it was conclusively shown in an extensive study performed in 2003 by Fenton-O'Creevy et al. that there is a strong inverse correlation between the degree to which a person experiences illusory control and their financial performance. In other words, the more you lose your mind to the market, the less rational your decisions will become, causing your investment performance to suffer ever more greatly. By all measures, including personal compensation, risk management, analytical abilities, and even people skills, among others, illusory control had a fairly strong negative impact (if you are the statistically-inclined type, the average r-squared for negative consequences resulting from illusory control was $-.25$, with r-squared of $-.33$ for the factors "profit contribution" and "risk management"). So, this very much qualifies as an environmentally-induced delusional disorder.

No one is completely immune to this, but not everyone responds as strongly as others. There are those among traders who do not experience illusory control quite so strongly, and there are some traders who go completely off the deep-end, comparing the experience as being like god. A person experiencing the delusion will likely not even notice it, themselves, but rather will need to have it pointed-out for them. Should that be the case, or if you wish to prevent illusory control within yourself before it takes-hold, then the best thing you can do is humble yourself. Now remember, people having severe problems with illusory control will experience disillusionment if you are successful in humbling them, and they may respond negatively to your intervention, so wear a helmet. It is a much less potentially painful thing to simply focus on humbling yourself

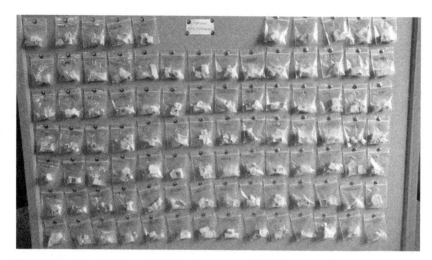

FIGURE 5.2 Operation Fuzzy Performance

rather than humble others (although there can be a great degree of schaden-freude in knocking some pretentious noise hole off their high horse). At any rate, for traders, this can really be quite a simple process: remember that over the long-run, on average your own performance is going to be far poorer than index funds. People are trusting you with their money, but the reality is that the best advice you could give them is to invest it themselves in funds which are completely unmanaged. Bummer, right? It gets better. Every now and then a study comes out – and you can perform these studies yourself – that compares the ability of some random nonsense to predict the stock market to top fund managers across the nation. As a bit of fun at the expense of fund managers, I performed an experiment of this type intended to be more ridiculous than normal. It was an experiment in the predictive powers of cheese in what I called "Operation Fuzzy Performance". See Fig. 5.2.

Using cheese to predict the future actually has a name: Tyromancy. The idea was inspired by a popular video game called The Witcher 3, and the cheese (a lovely double cream Gouda) was donated along with the baggies from The Cheese Lady in Traverse City, Michigan. Exactly 3 grams of cheese was placed into each of the bags, which were then sealed and affixed to corkboard. Then a list of all the stocks listed on major exchanges in the US were randomized using the RAND function in Excel, and the ticker symbol for the top 94 companies were written on the baggies, one ticker symbol per bag. There were a wide variety of industries, company sizes, and even nationalities involved, since ADRs were included in the sample. The board was then kept in a dark space at a constant temperature of 72 degree Fahrenheit. Starting with an imaginary $1 million the funds were allocated based on the volume of mold that grew on the cheese, the speed at which it grew, and which molds produced spores first. The allocations of investment funds were monitored and changed daily based on how quickly the mold matured and the volume of mold in each bag, with the $1 million being allocated more quickly to those molds which grew and matured more quickly, and a higher percentage of the total $1 million being allocated to the molds of greatest volume. The experiment began at the first signs of mold on April 18, 2017 and ended on May 22, 2017 once the mold began to produce clouds of orange spores inside the bags – their lifecycle had ended, and so did the experiment (and not a moment too soon, since you could practically feel the stink through your skin). The cheese performed admirably in its stock predictions. Based on an average performance of the S&P500, NASDAQ, and Dow Jones Industrial Average, during that period there was market growth of 2.79%, while the experimental cheese index saw an increase of 8.2% over the same period – outperforming each of the Top 25 US fund managers:

1) James Simons (Renaissance Tech)
2) Michael Platt (Bluecrest Capital)
3) Raymond Dalio (Bridgewater)
4) David Tepper (Appaloosa)
5) Kenneth Griffin (Citadel)
6) Daniel Loeb (Third Point)
7) Paul Singer (Elliott Management)
8) David Shaw (D.E. Shaw)
9) John Overdeck (Two Sigma)
10) David Siegel (Two Sigma)
11) Michael Hintze (CQS)
12) Jeffrey Talpins (Element Capital)
13) Stan Druckenmiller (Duquesne)
14) Brett Icahn (Icahn Capital)
15) David Schechter (Icahn Capital)
16) Christopher Hohn (Children's Investment Fund)
17) Seth Klarman (Baupost)
18) Israel Englander (Millennium)
19) Danny Yong (Dymon Asia)
20) Christopher Rokos (Rokos Capital)
21) Peter Muller (PDT)
22) Leon Cooperman (Omega)
23) Nelson Peltz (Trian)
24) Peter Brown (Renaissance Tech)
25) Bob Mercer (Renaissance Tech)

What it must feel like to be a globally-renowned investor when your predictions are beaten by moldy cheese. Notable mentions for stocks that grew mold quickly and produced spores early include Fortress Biotech which earned 19% over the time period, as well as CVR Energy (18%), and Magna International (14%). It should be noted that the cheese did miss big opportunities like Chegg and Secureworks Corp, though, both of which outperformed all the other stocks by far. Notable mentions for stocks that grew no mold at all, in some cases creating an airless vacuum within the bag, include Amyris which lost 52% of their value over the same time period, as well as Lantronix (28%) and Flotek Industries (14%). The cheese was quite wrong in recommending Tanger Factory Outlet Centers, though, even if only a small proportion of the total $1 million had been allocated to it. The average returns for the entire population of 94 stocks was 0.96%, which was 88% lower than the stocks which flourished with fluffy goodness. In the end, the cheese fund increase in value to $108,200.

Do realize I am not saying cheese can actually predict the future. It was pure dumb luck that the cheese did so well, actually, but simple experiments like these can go far in breaking the illusion that your investing decisions are even the slightest bit exceptional, since random events like mold growing on cheese can often do better.

5.6 MISPERCEIVED RISK

Mathematics is supposed to be certain – a discipline that works exclusively in absolutes and in which $2 + 2$ will always equal 4. At least, that is what people like to believe, so it tends to shake peoples' world a bit when they discover that one specific branch of mathematics, statistics and probability, is exactly the opposite. Rather than being the discovery of what we know, as with most maths, statistics is the discovery of what we do not know. This is precisely the reason that quantitative financial analysts and risk managers adore statistics – or at the very least you need to have a statistical background to get work in those career fields. Financial risk refers to the chance that an investment will lose value. If that loss of value was guaranteed and known, then it is no longer risk, it is merely a cost. So, in the world of investing, statistics is the language of risk, and investors use it to calculate the likelihood of incurring a cost, which is then translated into a "risk cost", which is simply the anticipated value of the cost multiplied by its percentage likelihood of occurring. In other words, if there is a chance you will lose $100 on an investment, and a 10% probability of that loss occurring based on your calculations (which will be invariably wrong), then the risk cost of that investment is $10. When you put that investment into a portfolio with a bunch of other investments, there are ways to manage the average risk of the portfolio to keep the chance of losses either below a certain percentage or below a given dollar threshold, or both. Again, though, it is all uncertainty, and even if you are 99% certain, there is still that 1% chance that you are wrong.

Do not worry, we are not going to delve into the mathematics of risk, because the reality is you are going to be wrong, anyway. It is not just you, either, it is everyone. No one on this planet has a fully comprehensive understanding of investment risk in general, or even the risks associated with a single stock. Sure, they can tell you what risk is and most of the time what they stand to lose (this becomes more difficult with investments into short selling, or trading in stock options), but accurately measuring the likelihood of a loss is not something which anyone can accurately do at the moment. It is something that is being actively worked on constantly, including some of my own research, but it there is no equation yet which allows us to fully understand all the factors that contribute to financial risk, much less how to utilize them. So, regardless of how much effort you put into convincing yourself that you know the risk inherent in an investment, your perception will still be quite different than the reality.

There are two broad categories of investment risk: Volatility risk and value risk. Volatility risk is of more interest to traders than investors, because if the market price of a particular stock is jumping around quite dramatically, then it is more difficult to predict movements accurately. Volatility does not inherently make a stock more risky, though. Despite what all the intro to investing books would have you believe, measures of volatility like beta and alpha don not actually measure risk – they only measure movement. By using beta, for example, you could look at a stock that is extremely consistent, barely changes at all, and perpetually loses money, yet it would be considered low risk because you are conflating risk and volatility. By contrast, value risk refers to measurements of a company's value, rather than its stock price. By looking at book value, source and quality of earnings, and things of that nature, then comparing them to the market price, you are measuring whether or not the stock price is too high compared to the company's value, creating a risk that the price will drop in the future. The truth is that the majority of quantitative analysts actually combine these, so that they are measuring the volatility of value risk in response to different factors, and their contributions to future market value.

There is also a much-overlooked aspect to risk which is qualitative in nature, rather than quantitatively measured using risk cost. For example, let us just say you have the option to either invest your money or repay your mortgage debt sooner. Sure, there is a chance you will earn greater returns on your investments than you are paying in debt interest, but exactly how certain are you that you are correct? Being homeless sucks, so is the potential reward on an investment high enough and reliable enough to make it worth risking homelessness? Sure, if the only thing you had to worry about was repaying the loan, and had no collateral at stake, then it is a much easier decision because you do not have to consider the reality that your quality of life will diminish significantly. So, that demonstrates how qualitative factors play into our assessment of risk – if an investment and debt have equal rates and risks, it is still worse to gamble with something that will impact your life, rather than simply reduce your financial performance. That actually poses a significant problem for professional investors, because they do not take these kinds of things into consideration. In fact, they cannot take these types of things into consideration most of the time, because they are often managing a pool of investment money from a variety of people with different life circumstances, or they do not know the people that are giving them investment money, or any number of factors.

The misperception of risk comes from three primary sources: ignorance, bias, or misdirected focus. Ignorance is the simplest to explain because it simply refers to the fact that we do not know what the hell we're doing, so our perceptions of risk are based on things that aren't actually measuring risk properly, resulting in insane decisions. The second source of risk misperception is bias. Like most biases, this means we are playing favorites in some way. "Availability bias" refers to a behavior in which we give newer information greater importance, regardless of reliability or validity. Other biases are more generic, wherein we place too much or too little importance on certain factors. For example, you may hear on the news that some politician or another is promising to build a massive wall which will cost billions, resulting in a dramatic increase in estimated future earnings for construction companies. By failing to realize that politicians are up to their eyeballs in bullshit, you would put place a greater probability of this occurring than reality, causing you to underestimate the amount of value risk in any investments you make in construction companies. The final source of misperceived risk is simply that you are basing your assessments of risk on the wrong thing. Just because banks are technically allowed to lend a high percentage of their available cash to borrowers as determined by the Federal Reserve Bank decreasing the reserve ratio (the amount of total deposits they have to keep on-hand) does not necessarily mean it is a good idea. Even if a bank keeps more cash in reserve than necessary, they are still focusing only on a regulatory reference point for risk, rather than the quality of their loans and their need for cash to maintain normal operations.

There is no escaping misperceived risk. The best thing you can do to help prevent it from effecting your investing decisions in a negative way is to get multiple opinions. If each person has their own misperceptions, then it is likely that you will find people who do not share your same perception of risk, and can challenge your perceptions. By forcing yourself to defend what you think is true, you can help to better find a better way of seeing things.

5.7 ROLE OF EXPECTATIONS

This section is going to be short because there is not much to say about the role of expectations in investing behavior. It is basically the stock market version of the placebo effect – People believe something will happen, so it does. For example, if people simply believe that the market is going to crash, then even if there is no cause for it, the market will crash because everyone withdraws their money from the market in anticipation of a crash that otherwise would not have occurred. If something happens in politics or society that would make people believe a certain type of product or service will see a sudden increase in demand, then people will rush to buy stocks in that industry causing the market price of the stocks to rise even if nothing would have actually happened. At first it would seem that this is related to herd behavior (discussed in Chapter 4.1), but there is something distinctly different about the role of expectations that makes it more a matter of perception than behavior.

Self-fulfilling prophecies have been the bane of human existence at least since the days of Oedipus. The simplest example comes from the Great Depression, when people expected that the banks would run out of money, so those people began with withdrawal all their money from the accounts actually causing the banks to run out of money (something called a "bank run"). Had that expectation not been established in their minds, then the banks could have maintained enough of their cash reserves to remain in operation. Instead, banks were forced to freeze accounts. A modern version of self-fulfilling prophecy comes from an urban legend or superstition in Hong Kong. Adam Cheng is an actor who starred in the 1992 show The Greed of Man, which is about unscrupulous stock market behaviors. That same year, the Hong Kong market experienced a crash, and people blamed it on the film, especially the primary bad guy named Ting Hai, played by Adam Cheng. Since then, anytime a movie or show is released starring Adam Cheng, the Hong Kong stock market drops. The two things clearly have nothing to do with each other, but because it has become an urban legend, people alter their investing behaviors, whether they even realize it or not. It happens simply because people believe it will, and even if investors try to ignore it the Ting Hai Effect as superstitious nonsense, the fact that the markets tend to drop make even the most skeptical investors more risk averse simply as a result of the self-fulfilling prophecy. The mere perception that something will occur actually makes that thing occur. People have an expectation, and cause it to become a reality because they act upon that expectation irrationally.

The good news is that not only can you protect yourself against the role of expectations in investing, but you can use it to your advantage. Start by remaining skeptical and reminding yourself that just because you think something will happen does not mean it will. Instead of merely expecting something to happen, focus on whether or not you have any evidence it will happen, and whether or not that evidence has validity, or has been reliable in the past. Do not act on something unless you have sound reasoning. However, if you come to find that there is sound reasoning to expect something to happen based purely on the irrational expectations of others, then you can take advantage of that knowledge. If you are fully convinced that the Ting Hai effect is valid, then by simply checking to see what projects Adam Cheng is working on and what the release dates will be, you can sell your stocks shortly before the release date and then rebuy them once the market drops in response to that release.

5.8   FRAME MANIPULATION

Throughout this chapter we have covered a lot of different ways your brain messes-up your perception of the world around you, resulting in bizarre investing behaviors. In the end, though, they can all be attributed, in varying degrees, to your psychological frame. Your frame is composed of everything that makes you who you are: your experiences, your memories, your beliefs, your knowledge set, your emotional state, your culture, your ideas, and everything else. There are external factors that compose your frame, including the environment in which you grew-up, your degree of education, influential experiences in your life, and so forth. There are also internal factors that shape your frame, such as your degree of emotional volatility, your ability to recall events, your self-image, your genetically-driven propensity to behave in certain ways, and things of that nature. When you look at the events of the world around you, all these things contribute to the way you perceive them, understand them, and respond to them. That is why it is called a psychological frame: It is the structure and state of your mind through which you view the world.

To put it a bit more concisely, psychological framing is the process by which a person observes, interprets, and responds to an event within the context of their understanding, which is shaped by their knowledge and past experiences. Knowing this, we can talk about frame analysis, wherein you study a person to identify the things which compose that person's frame and the impact that their frame has on their behaviors. We do this all the time without even realizing it, and it is not as complex of a process as it sounds. Think about it within the context of any conversation – as you talk to each other, each of you are trying to determine what the other person wants to accomplish, what motivates them, why they say or do certain things; and generally trying to discover whether you have mutual interests, whether you can trust each other, whether the other person will respond positively the your own words and actions, and so forth. We are doing this on a constant basis, even around the people close to us. We care about what our friends and family think, so we weigh our words and actions, and we do this by understanding the things about each person that shape how they will interpret what you say and how they will respond to that interpretation. The best politicians and networkers are constantly and actively analyzing the frames of the people around them to understand how to interact with each person in the way that is most productive. The problem, though, is that each of us have our own frames, as well, so everything we know about the people around us is shaped by those things which shape our own behaviors. That is where miscommunication comes from. A person might say something that is benign within their own experiences, but someone with another frame could be entirely insulted by it. The simplest examples of this are found in vulgarities of verbal and non-verbal actions. When I was teaching economics in Beijing, it was quite a shock when a group of students associated with some club or another came to school all wearing shirts that just said "FUCK" on them. They knew the word was considered a vulgarity in the English language, but since they were not raised in a culture whose history has placed such significance on the word, nobody thought anything about it. At the same time, if I were to write some Chinese vulgarities in this chapter, you would know intellectually that it was a vulgar word only because I told you, so you would not have the same kind of emotional or visceral response that you do to my use of English vulgarities.

As a side note, children who speak English will giggle when they hear that there is a lake called "Titicaca", because of the words and images they associated with the way it is pronounced. Those same kids would not think much about the Gobi Desert, although children who speak Mandarin Chinese will giggle at it because it basically means "Dog Penis" Desert. There are many adults in each nation who will giggle just like children when hearing about these places if they are around close friends or family, because of the contribution of context to the frames of the people around them. By contrast, while in a business meeting, the contribution of context to a person's frame would prevent them from responding in such a manner.

This is where we get to the fun part, and finally bring all this back to investing behaviors. This is where we start talking about frame manipulation. Once you understand the factors that influence a person's frame, you can present information to them in ways that are intended to illicit a specific response. In fact, a variety of studies (which, for some gruesome reason, often involve runaway trains and death tolls – maybe economics is a dismal science) have shown that the way information is presented is more important than the information, itself. These studies give you surveys and you have to make decisions about who lives and dies, then will later-on give you a scenario with the exact same outcomes but worded in a different manner. Believe it or not, even though the actual information being presented in these scenarios are identical, people changed their answers based on how the scenarios were worded.

Here is a simple example to demonstrate how this works:

Scenario 1) The market price of Company X's stock is only 25% of its previous year's price, making it a cheap buy with great potential!

Scenario 2) The market price of Company X's stock has dropped by 75% over the past year, making it extremely volatile and far too risky.

In both these scenarios, the exact same information is being presented – only the way it is being presented has changed. If you were not aware of frame manipulation, then it is almost guaranteed that you would make your decision of whether to invest in Company X or not based on which version of these events you heard, rather than the events, themselves. Oh, we like to think that financial decisions are all rational, calculated decisions based on carefully-developed quantitative measurements, but this clearly demonstrates that two people looking at the same mathematical data can come to two very separate conclusions about the potential risk and reward of a specific investment.

This sort of frame manipulation happens all the time in financial journalism, news, and blogs. Sometimes it is intentional, wherein some jackass guest "expert" will appear to talk about the status of one company or another, and the entire time they have every intention of manipulating market price for their own purposes. They are not outright lying, necessarily, but the way they provide this information is manipulative as hell. Other times, the journalist is not doing it on purpose – what they learned about a stock was given to them by someone else, who learned about it from their own sources, and so forth until you get to original jackass who has a stake in ensuring the public responds to financial information in a particular way.

The impact of your psychological frame on investing decisions is not always so overtly obvious, either. In a study I did back in 2017, I demonstrated conclusively that there was a relationship between cultural uncertainty avoidance and investment risk aversion. Based on nothing more than the geographic location of where you were raised, it is possible to state that the investors in your nation, on average, are interpreting the degree of risk associated with standardized metrics like alpha and beta in a different manner than the people in another country. The reason is simple: Different nations have different levels of uncertainty avoidance – culturally, people in some nations tend to be more accepting of uncertainty, while in other nations people tend to want to ensure everything is planned and known in advance. Less uncertainty avoidance means less risk aversion in equity investments. Culture, the social customs and behaviors in which a person is raised, is a large part of a person's psychological frame, and as that frame develops it will determine the investing decisions made later in life.

CONCLUSION

You most likely noticed that the different topics discussed in this chapter have a lot in common, and all share similar traits. Several of them can be tied to prospect theory, while others are tied to differences in the information available between people. In the end, though, they are all the result of our own psychological frames. The information we have available to us is part of our frame, and shapes how we perceive the world around us, the accuracy of our risk assessments, and our degree of advantages in situations of information asymmetry. The way we respond to potential losses and potential gains results from how comfortable we are with these things, and the perception of differences in value between loss and gain. Everything we perceive is done through a frame of our own understanding of the world, shaped by experiences, knowledge, genetics, culture, and more. How we view the world depends entirely on who we are, making the very nature of the world a relative thing. No wonder we cannot even agree on investing behavior – something which is supposed to be quantitative and rational – as people come to totally separate conclusions looking at the exact same numbers. Not even the use of statistics can save us when the data we are analyzing means different things to different people. How mad must we be that nothing is true?

Chapter 6

Feeling Foolish

If you are happy, then you are wrong. If you are sad, then you are also wrong. If you are angry, tired, lonely, excited, anxious, surprised, joyful, disgusted, envious, indignant, shameful, afraid, ecstatic, pensive, or feeling anything else at all, then you are wrong. Your emotions make you weak... well, at the very least they are harming your investing decisions by making you less rational. So, let us take a lesson from Mr. Spock and purge ourselves of all emotion so that we may approach our investments logically, but be careful not to take it too far and lose your sense of emotional response altogether, entering the realm of psychopathy – we will visit that in Chapter 7.

6.1 EMOTIONAL INFLUENCE

Investors, and traders in particular, are a skittish bunch. They act confident so long as they can hide behind a smokescreen of calculations, graphs, and data; but all of it is just that: a simple smokescreen which fails to hide their deeper instincts. Even the slightest bit of news, good or bad, will influence a person's entire investing strategy for a time, regardless of whether it is relevant. Tornado hits Oklahoma? Well, then surely we must be careful and avoid any investing risk. The smoking hot barista at the coffee shop you go to every day smiled and winked at you this morning? You probably feel like you could charge headlong into open combat with your bare fists and come out of it a hero... that is, at least until you realize investment portfolio lost 10% of its value the next day because you were acting like an idiot. All that bouncing around you see when you look at a graph of stock prices has a lot less to do with assessing value or identifying autocorrelative trends in the market, and more to do with how people are feeling from moment to moment. Keep a close eye on a major news network one week (preferably one that investors typically watch, like CNBC, or reading the Wall Street Journal, or other sources with an emphasis on finance), and watch the streaming data of a major stock index like DJIA or S&P 500. You will find that the stock markets will either jump or drop, slightly but consistently, in response to the tone of the news at any given time. If some bad things have happened, the stock market will drop, regardless of whether or not any of the individual companies listed on that market are actually effected. If there is good news, then investor sentiment will improve, causing the market value to improve. It is a truly bizarre thing to realize that the decisions that supposedly determine the outcome of the retirements for so many people, and which decide how financial

Market Insanity. DOI: 10.1016/B978-0-12-813115-2.00006-9

capital is allocated across the world to drive economic growth, are all partially the result of whether somebody woke-up grumpy or not.

Ok, proof. That is a big assertion to make, and one that defies the assumptions made by economists and financial professionals for more than a century. So, if I am going to claim that they have all been deluding themselves into thinking that they are more rational than they really are, then there must be some kind of evidence, right? Right! It all begins with Robert Shiller, who is one of those superstars in the economics world. We already discussed how his research shattered any illusions people had that the market responded efficiently or rationally to market forces, but that does not prove that emotional responses are contributing to the problem. In 1984, part of Shiller's work included collecting data from investors on what motivated them to make their investing decisions at a given point in time. This has been done continuously since 1989 and the results have been very conclusive, resulting in the development of a brand new type of investing measurement: investor confidence. There are several of these measurements on US stock markets alone, including measurements of confidence that stocks will increase in value over the next 1 year period, whether stocks will rebound after a sudden downturn (called the Buy-on-Dips Index), and the degree of confidence that the market will not crash in the next 6 months. These indices are now widely used and have proven to be quite reliable in explaining much of the movement in the markets that could not be explained by people making rational decisions.

Since then, Shiller has focused his work largely on the matter of investment bubbles (which were also discussed in Chapter 4.1) and the role that the overconfident investor has to play in creating them. He has predicted several investment bubbles successfully as a result of his research, not only in the stock market but only in the real estate markets. This is supported by more recent research performed by University College, London in 2008 which concluded that, "Investors get carried away with excitement and wishful fantasies as the stock market soars, suppressing negative emotions which would otherwise warn them of the high risk of what they are doing." This is a common behavior seen in auctions, as well, wherein people bidding on an object will get swept-up in the excitement and the competition that they will completely lose themselves and end-up paying far too much for an item than it was actually worth.

This does not just apply to bubbles and excitement, either. No, the stock market clearly is not all unicorns and rainbows, as demonstrated by Barber, Odean, and Strahilevitz, in a 2011 paper that studied 66,465 investor accounts between 1991 and 1996, then another 596,314 accounts from 1997 until 1999. The results of their study? "Having sold a stock, investors are disappointed if it continues to rise and regret having sold it in the first place. They anticipate that their disappointment and regret will be more intense if they repurchase such a stock rather than not repurchasing it; thus investors are most likely to repurchase a stock previously sold for a gain that is trading below the price at which they sold it." In other words, rebuying a stock at a higher price than they sold it is a bit like adding insult to injury, so instead of just admitting their mistake and getting rebuying a stock that is performing well, people will avoid that stock completely unless its price dips back down below the price they originally sold it. In the 4th century CE, the monk Evagrius Ponticus listed pride as one of the 7 deadly since, and in all this time people still have failed to learn to ignore their pride if it leads them to act irrationally.

Sometimes you are told to listen to your emotions – to "trust your gut" or "listen to your heart" – but when it comes to investing, that is really bad advice. Lo, Repin, and Steenbarger published a study with the National Bureau of Economic Research in 2005 that measured the emotional response of professional day-traders using standard physiological measurements like hear rate, respiration, perspiration, etc. They found, quite conclusively, that "subjects whose emotional reaction to monetary gains and losses was more intense on both the positive and negative side exhibited significantly worse trading performance." It does appear that not all investors are equally effected by the burning passions within them, though (I never thought I would use "investors" and "burning passions" in the same sentence). Prior to the 2005 paper, Lo and Repin did another project in 2002 which proved that investors respond emotionally to market behaviors, and that their investing decisions suffer as a result. We already discussed that, though. The 2002 paper was unique in that it showed that more experienced investors were less influenced by market behaviors, tending to respond most strongly to periods of high volatility, while inexperienced traders were more emotionally responsive and that they responded to a broader range of market behaviors. Now, remember, it is easy to come to the conclusion that experience makes people more rational, but this could just as easily indicate that people who are less rational tend to quit, so that the only traders who last long enough to become experienced are those who can keep a level head under pressure.

Finally, here is a study that the women will love to hear. In 2015, Harding and he performed a study on the impact of negative mood has on investing behavior. As described in the beginning of this chapter, they did find that a deterioration in a person's mood resulted in an increase in risk aversion. A bad mood prevents people from taking risks even when it is warranted, while being in a good mood, particularly an overly good mood, makes people take excessive risk. What is unique about these findings, though, was that this emotional volatility was only found in men, while women did not appear to change their investing behaviors as a result of their mood. To my knowledge, this is the only study that even tried to tackle that topic, so more research is probably needed before speculating on the "how" and "why" of these results.

Regardless of whose investing behaviors are effected by their emotions more strongly or why, the fact remains that our emotions do have a significant influence on our investing behavior. So, is there anything we can do to limit that and become more rational? I am afraid the answer is "no". Even if you use a pre-programmed algorithm, you are still programming your own neuroses into it –

or the neuroses of whoever developed it. Even if you diversify your portfolio, the composition and management of that portfolio will still be influenced by your emotions. As Kristina Zucchi suggests for Investopia.com, dollar-cost averaging may help, but she is wrong. Dollar-cost averaging simply means buying the same dollar amount of a particular investment at fixed intervals, regardless of what the market is doing. Pursuing this strategy does not eliminate emotional influence on your investing strategy, this strategy is entirely the result of emotional influence. To continue investing in something over time regardless of what is happening is a preposterous proposition to ponder, and has been shows in multiple studies to generally be a piss-poor investing strategy. The reason it is pursued or recommended at all is as a result of fear – fear of entering the market too quickly. As we have already shown, negative emotions result in poorer performance, so that this strategy fails is no surprise. At any rate, the very nature of this strategy ends-up being sheer torture for the investors. As they are pursuing this strategy out of fear of investing in the market in a manner consistent with the analytics, they will then get to watch as every investment period they purchase fewer shares of stocks that are succeeding, and more shares of stocks that are failing. As noted throughout Chapter 5, people are more averse to loss than they are attracted to gain, so this strategy exaggerates that phenomenon, resulting in periods of feeling minor success while their investments are increasing, and utter emotional devastation during periods of loss.

Best advice: Just work on keeping a cool head. Meditate, take some deep breaths, or do whatever it is you have to in order to find a calm headspace where you find your inner tranquility… or inner sociopath… or inner Spock.

6.2 GAMBLER'S FALLACY

Behavioral economists really like casinos. There are just so many people who are already participating in things which have known probabilities that it gives us an excuse to go to places like Las Vegas, Monte Carlo, Macau, and other places and it is still considered valid work for which we get paid! In fact, some of the most profound advancements in the statistics used by economists have been discovered in casinos. So, on behalf of statisticians and economists everywhere, let me thank you for making our job a lot of fun from time to time. In return, I would like to share with you a bit of information that you need to hear – you will not like it, but it will help you both in the stock market and in the casinos: You are making dumb decisions.

That is not the helpful part, though. The thing you need to know is that the Gambler's Fallacy is real, it takes several forms, and it is hardwired into your brain in a serious way, so you odds are you have made this fallacy and not even realize it. Like all fallacies, the Gambler's Fallacy results from a failure to understand or a failure to apply proper logic. Another common fallacy is the ad hominem fallacy, in which people who disagree with each other will say nasty things about each other as a way to try to prove them wrong, when the reality is that whether a person's argument is correct or not has nothing to do with who that person actually is or what they have done (the reverse of this scenario is extremely common in academia, wherein a person will cite their academic and professional credentials as a reason for being correct, when the truth is that such arguments only prove the person is completely full of themselves, rather than actually being correct). By contrast, the Gambler's Fallacy comes from improper logic related not to a person, but to the likelihood of something occurring – a faulty assessment of probability.

This can occur in several different ways. The most common example takes place at the roulette wheel (the table with the round spinny thing with all the red and black numbers on it). A person could bet on black over and over and over, and lose each time, but they will tell themselves that since it has been red so many times, then it is due to land on black this next time. According to a 2004 book by David Darling, in August 18, 1913 there was a roulette table in Monte Carlo which landed on black 26 times in a row, resulting in substantial losses for gamblers who were left in disbelief. The logical error they made was that they assumed that just because something had occurred several times in a row, that it somehow changed the likelihood of the next spin. The reality is that no matter how many times you spin a roulette wheel, there is also a 50% chance of landing on black and a 50% chance of landing on red (ignoring the green 00 space in which no one wins).

Another variation of this fallacy is often associated with the phrase "let it ride!" That means a person has won, and intends to bet on that same color of the wheel again. That is fine, but the fallacy comes into play when a person comes to believe that since the wheel has landed on black so many times, that it is destined to land on black again in the next spin because there is a trend, or that the individual gambler is "on a hot streak" (i.e.: they are doing well). This is called the "clustering illusion", wherein it appears that an outcome must be more likely because it is associated with similar recent outcomes. Again, probability does not work that way. While it is true that if you spin the wheel an infinite number of times, you will get an equal frequency of both blacks and reds, but that is based on averages. Each individual spin still has the same probability of outcome, no matter how far from the average the game seems to deviate.

One final variation of this logical fallacy is when a person comes to believe that an unlikely event must have come from a long series of attempts. For example, if you bet on a single number at the roulette wheel, there is only a 2.63% chance that you will win that spin. However, even though the odds are low, they will be equal for every spin. As a result, you are just as likely to win the first time you try it, as you are likely to win the 1000th time. The probability does not change based on your persistence or fate or anything else – it is just random probability.

The cause of the Gambler's Fallacy is most widely accepted by research performed by (once again) Kahneman and Tversky. They attribute the fallacy to one or both of two different distortions in logic. The first is the "belief in small numbers", as they call it, which basically states that people really believe that deviations from the average must eventually correct themselves during the period in which they are standing at that table. Yes, it is true that mathematically speaking, any deviations from the mean will correct itself, but when we are talking about mathematics we are also dealing with impossibly gigantic numbers, or limits such as infinity. So, even observing several hundred spins of the table will not necessarily give you the correction you seek so badly. The second cause of the Gambler's Fallacy, according to Kahneman and Tversky stems from representativeness heuristics. Ok, first of all, heuristics refers to the way we learn and make decisions – specifically, they are little shortcuts we develop to make estimations of the correct answer, but which fail to rigorously prove that something is correct. Representativeness heuristics, as a result, refers to peoples' tendency to estimate the probability of something based on its similarity to experiences they have observed in the past. Sadly, all heuristics are subject to error and make people prone to making fallacies or forming biases, and the flaws associated with representativeness heuristics contribute to the stereotypes that people create about each other based on what they have seen in the news or hear from other people. After terror attacks in the US or London by Islamic extremists, people in these nations saw an upsurge in anti-Muslim sentiment because they came to believe that these isolated incidents were representative of all Muslims. The reality is that there are more terror attacks performed by Christians in the US than by Muslims, but flaws in our mental reasoning do not allow many people to accept that as fact.

Representativeness heuristics, as applied to the Gambler's Fallacy, refers to a person's tendency to look for trends or patterns, and use their past observations to estimate future outcomes of the roulette wheel. There is extensive research demonstrating that people find trends and patterns where they do not exist, going as far as to actually create sensory illusions such as those used by magicians. People tend to see faces and shapes in things where they do not actually exist, develop conspiracies or superstitions based on a series of unrelated events which were, at best, coincidental. This pattern-seeking behavior is extremely deeply embedded in our minds, thought to have evolved in response to avoiding predators (i.e.: the person who is more prone to run from nothing will pass-on their genes, while the person who stays and gets eaten does not). Our daily lives require us to find patterns and make assumptions about what will occur, otherwise every step we take would be a terrifying gamble of whether or not the ground would stay solid below our feet. These examples are all based on heuristics, however, and so representativeness heuristics is greatly supported as the most likely culprit in our attempts to find and apply patterns which do not exist to matters of financial risk.

Investing is not the same as gambling, at all. Gambling is done as a game of pure chance, with the expectancy that you will likely lose money (the casino almost always has the statistical advantage, and even in those times where you can find a statistical advantage for yourself, I speak from experience when I say the casino still has the advantage of being able to forcefully escort your ass to the nearest concrete ground outside of casino property). By contrast, investing is ideally done with a degree of knowledge and reasonable expectations that you will make more money than you lose. Still, that does not stop people from making the same mistakes as gamblers.

The effect of the Gambler's fallacy on investors is the same reason this topic was included in the chapter regarding emotional influence, rather than the chapter on perception. Specifically, since a person cannot justify the decisions they make based on the Gambler's fallacy, it is always expressed as a "feeling" or a "gut instinct". Investors who buy a stock that drops in price will continue to hold onto that stock because they just become obsessed with the idea that it will have to eventually increase in price again, so that they can at least resell it for the price they bought it (which, of course, is ridiculous, since they would continue to hold onto that stock if it was increasing in price, since they now believe it is increasing in value like they originally thought it would). It is typical for investors with well-diversified portfolios to invest in a random assortment of highly speculative stocks, with the belief that if they just invest in enough of them at least one of them has to succeed. There is no reason to believe that, though, other than sometimes a speculative stock does do very well, but unless you know about the individual company and have a valid reason to think it will succeed, you are more likely to get swindled by some shell corporation that raises capital and immediately shuts-down. Despite this, far too many investors feel the strong enticement try their luck, without validating the investing decisions they are making beyond applying trends in portfolio statistics improperly. It is quite common for a company to perform well one period, and investors will see that then immediately invest in that company or other companies within the same industry, without considering whether or not there is reason to believe that the individual company or any other company in the industry will continue to perform so well. To the contrary, it is nearly impossible for a company to sustain any rapid rate of growth for an extended period of time. If a company worth $1 million increases in value by 10% in a single year, then it will be worth $1.1 million, which is $100,000 more than the previous year. In order to sustain that 10% growth rate they cannot just make another $100,000, they would have to make $ 110,000, which is 10% more than they made before. This quickly turns into an impossibly fast rate of growth. That does not stop investors from jumping to conclusions, though.

In order to minimize the effects of the Gambler's fallacy on your investing, first start with a functional approach, by assessing your investments strictly at their spot metrics – the value and risk at any given point in time. Doing so will help you to be able to validate your decisions by assessing whether an investment makes sense based strictly on its current financial and operational health. Rather than being concerned with patterns and probabilities, assess each investment based on its value and risk. Have a justified reason to believe that an investment will increase or decrease in value, other than simple historical patterns.

Although carefully assessing the validity of your investment decisions based on things other than patterns can be helpful, there are two important flaws with it. First of all, it is really extremely difficult to prevent your brain from seeking-out patterns. Gestalt psychologists have demonstrated that we will actually see things that are not that, at all, just because we are looking for patterns. Need proof? Very gently use your finger and set it to the outside edge of your eye, and carefully press it toward your nose. While doing that, place your attention out the corner of your other eye. You see that round blank spot? That blank spot is always there – it is perpetually in our vision, but we do not see it because our brain automatically fills-in the blank spot. The second problem with assessing your investments for value rather than pattern, is that patterns really do exist in the stock market. By ignoring historical performance, or annual growth trends, or changes in the amount of cash a company has available to pay their bills, you are ignoring an absolutely vital part of any financial analysis. I could tell you to look for patterns but just be careful those patterns are real, but you are going to find patterns everywhere, then. It is unavoidable. So, in order to supplement your attempts to validate an investment using strictly value and risk metrics, try looking at events individually rather than as a series. Even if the events truly are part of a series or are otherwise related, it is a good mental exercise to break-down each event and assume it is isolated, then assess how that assumption would change your decision. This will allow you to override your brain's tendency to see patterns everywhere, and identify what is truly relevant and what is a mental illusion. As an added bonus, this will also help you better understand the nature of your decision-making process and identify ways to improve your investing decisions.

6.3 MOTIVATIONAL THEORY

Your alarm clock goes-off; the same blaring electronic buzz that has brought you to a half-conscious stupor every weekday for the last several years. You have learned to despise it just as much as you rely on it to ensure you make it to work on time, but work has grown tedious and burdensome, and in your semi-lucid state you can see no reason to bother yourself with it today. So, you turn-off the alarm, push it off your bedside table into the trash can sitting on the other side, and roll back onto your side, hoping to revisit that dream you were having of diving into the world's biggest taco. Then, only minutes later, you awake again with eyes wide open, and in a near panic. It is not the alarm calling out to you this time. No, this time it is your bladder. Since you were now awake anyway, you decided you may as well go to work in order to keep the collection companies off your back.

In our little example, could you identify where motivation came from? Do you think the example illustrates an individual who will be driven to perform

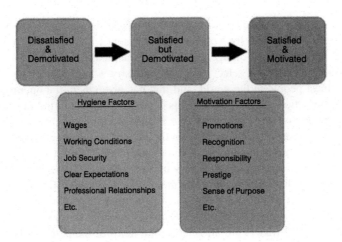

FIGURE 6.1 Herzberg's Two-Factor Theory

well and thrive in their career, or are they more likely to do their job just well-enough to ensure they keep drawing a paycheck (for more on that, see Chapter 4.5)? What factors did you identify that contributed to the lack of motivation for one's work? What did you notice about the dream, or the panicked rush to the restroom that provide indications of what drive us to be either satisfied or even singularly obsessed with achieving their goals to the fullest?

To help answer these questions, let us take a look at Fig. 6.1, which illustrates Herzberg's Two-Factor Theory of Motivation, developed in 1959.

According to this theory, there are those things we experience which keep up going for the sake of our continued survival, but these things do not drive us to excel in our pursuits. These things are called Hygiene Factors, named as such because they are external to the work, itself, and are used to maintain proper operations since the threat of their removal will cause dissatisfaction or discomfort to the lives of the employees, keeping them moving. Hygiene factors do not, however, give a person the opportunity to take ownership and responsibility for their career – they do not give them a sense of opportunity and purpose derived from the accomplishments they achieve within their work. These are the things which motivate people to thrive in the workplace, which is why they are known as "motivation factors".

The industry of professional or full-time investing is unique in that everything about it emphasizes a single hygiene factor: Money. The majority of the population are not so inclined to manage their own investments full-time, nor to become a full-time investor. The majority of the population has not even read a book or taken a seminar on personal finance. They are not motivated to improve their literacy of financial management, so instead they place their finances in the hands of financial advisers, fund managers, and others in the investing field with the hopes that they will earn enough money to sustain them but without having to do any of the work, themselves. As for the investors, themselves, the stock market is heavily regulated not only by law, but by the nature of the industry, itself. There is little room for a person to experiment with innovative new ideas, or to receive recognition of any sort, because the nature of the job is the same for everyone. There are a select few in the industry who have become some of the wealthiest people in the world, and that has given them the opportunity to achieve recognition and prestige, but this is extremely rare. For the vast majority of professional investors, the best they can hope for is to attract new clients and make enough money that they can open their own firm, at which point they are still doing the same type of work but now they are the boss instead of the employee. The stock market is also a very unforgiving environment that is highly competitive, so job security is far from guaranteed, and the professional interactions you make tend to be very "cutthroat" rather than developing healthy bonds – so there is a very high turnover rate among investors and traders. New professional investors/traders are attracted to the field for the potential of earning a large salary. It is true that working in the stock market can be very lucrative, but even that is not guaranteed, as pay is very often based on performance, so every potential client who rejects your offer to represent their financial interests represents your failure to earn that income, while every stock transaction you make will be heavily scrutinized to determine what it contributes to your salary. As quoted by famous investor Warren Buffet, "Wall Street is the only place that people ride to in a Rolls Royce to get advice from those who take the subway." Not only is the primary attraction to working on the stock market something of an illusory dream, but the nature of the work itself it helping others make income, so their efforts are not even put toward something that would motivate others. There is a total lack of healthy hygiene or motivational drive within the working environment of the stock market.

This is supported by another theory of motivation (which, as I've argued in some of my other books should be looked at as more of a theory of morale than motivation), known as Maslow's Pyramid of Needs, seen in Fig. 6.2.

The core functions of working in the stock market, as already noted, are limited in nature and emphasize consistency and conformity of service. Clearly, people working on the stock market can meet all their physiological needs, though the psychological strain can interrupt a person's ability to sleep and have sexual relations (see Chapter 7.2 for more on that). The remainder of the needs listed in Maslow's Pyramid are only questionably available at best, and nearly impossible to achieve at worst. That is to say, this maintains true within the core functions of the work.

When people have low morale and little which is truly a healthy source of motivation, they care less about the proper way to perform their work. The job, itself, has little meaning or purpose, so people, by their very nature, will look for ways to find motivation and improve their morale. In other words, they will find ways to be creative in their work, and in the stifling atmosphere of the stock market, this very often leads to behaviors which are less than desirable. For investors, this may come in the form of excessive risk-taking in the

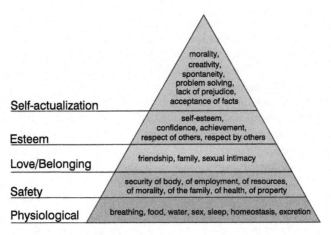

FIGURE 6.2 Maslow's Pyramid

hopes of achieving accomplishments and recognition. It may take the form of increased trading activity, instead of managing long-term investments, in order to stay active and challenge one's self. It can take the form of experimenting with investing strategies which are unorthodox or otherwise perform less than optimally simply for the sake of curiosity and discovery. For example, in recent years we have seen a dramatic upswing in the number of "activist investors". These individuals typically pursue one of two methods; either they invest in companies based on the contributions the company intends to make to society or the environment, or they will invest in companies operating in ways that are deemed harmful and use their influence as shareholders to impose changes on their operations. In either case, while these people may have noble intentions, it does tend to impede their performance as investors by decreasing returns. I could not find the transcripts, but on the radio there was an interview with… I think it was Jim Cramer, who asserted that if you want to be an activist investor, then be a successful investor and use your gains to pursue your causes. The example given was in the tobacco industry, which the interviewee predicted was going to be very successful in the future, stating that if the person did not like to tobacco industry then they should invest in companies which function within that industry and earn money from their success which can then be used to fight them in other ways.

Focusing less on the investing function, itself, professionals will also entertain new ways to achieve what they seek from their clients, by phishing for recognition to improve their esteem, or by overstating what they can achieve. In a worst-case scenario, this can lead to illegal behavior by making promises of returns which are impossible to sustain, and paying those returns with the investment money of others, developing what is known as a Ponzi scheme. Finding creative ways to acquire insider information can be quite satisfying, allowing a person to express their creativity, feel a strong sense of accomplishment when succeeding, and all while introducing a bit of added excitement into their lives. It is also common for investors to find a sense of satisfaction in superiority of status by spending as much time with their wealthiest clients as possible and getting to experience their lifestyle, all while neglecting other clients and allowing those investments to stagnate.

The matter of motivation also brings-up a significant agency problem. In other words, the professional acting on behalf of their clients has different motivations than the clients, themselves, leading the professional functioning poorly as an agent of their clients. It is, of course, the goal of a financial professional to get paid, and to appear financially successful, themselves, otherwise why should clients believe they are capable investors? The problem with this is that professional investors have a very common tendency to pursue behaviors which motivate themselves, such as maximizing their own income, gambling (see Chapter 6.2) on the stock market, and otherwise ignoring the majority of their clients to give the most attention to their wealthiest clients, among a variety of other issues which may arise.

Motivational factors are universal to everyone, even if the exact factors that impact us most vary from person to person. To ensure that your investing activities are not influenced in a negative manner by the things which motivate you, it is necessary to both separate our own personal motivations from our work activities as best as possible, and to align our motivations with those of our clients. This is not very difficult to achieve, but you must ensure that professional success in your job is your primary goal. Success for your clients will bring success for you, as well, as the metrics upon which your success is measured improve, and happy clients bring you additional potential clients, increasing your total earnings. You can then use the earnings you acquire through the pure pursuit of income rather than other motivational or hygiene factors to pursue things which give you a sense of achievement, belonging, and purpose. By simply remaining mindful that your investing career is a means to an end, you can align more rational investing behaviors in your mind with the things that drive you, allowing you to better thrive in the workplace.

It can also be helpful to remain aware of Temporal Motivational Theory, which states that motivation is equal to (expectancy multiplied by value) divided by (1 plus impulsiveness multiples by delay). The underlying concept here is how much a person craves instant gratification. The longer a person must wait, and the more impulsive that person is, the less they will be motivated to wait for greater returns. This, in itself, is entirely irrational behavior, but it does help to explain the divide between value investors and volume traders, and it also helps to define the irrational behaviors which investors tend to exhibit as described in this chapter on motivational theory. Generating lower returns as a result of impatience seems like a newbie mistake, but it is extremely common. Being mindful of your impulses by emphasizing your focus on the value you expect to earn, and emphasizing patience in pursuing the greatest returns, in may just help you increase the rationality of your investment decisions.

6.4 PSYCHOLOGICAL REWARD

It is that rush, that feeling of intense euphoria and excitement that you get which drives you to take it further and further just to get the same experience, until it all comes crashing down around you and you find yourself begging for just a little taste to get normal again. Make no doubt about it, it will come crashing down, and when it does you will feel less than you did before you started this nonsense in the first place, so you get back up on your feet and start over, working to feel that rush once more.

What do you think: Confessions of a cocaine addict or the regular experience of being a professional investor? The truth is that it could be either, and the two actually have a lot of parallels, psychologically. In fact, according to a 2001 study by Breiter, Aharon, Kahneman (geez, this guy is everywhere), Dale, and Shizgal, "It is striking that the activations seen in [nucleus accumbens], [sublenticular extended amygdala], [ventral tegmental dopamine neurons], and [orbitofrontal cortex] in response to monetary prospects and outcomes overlap those observed in response to cocaine infusions in subjects addicted to cocaine."

If you're not aware, the nucleus accumbens is the part of the brain that processes reward stimuli and aversion stimuli, as well as reinforcing stimuli, such as the need to eat or drink. So this part of the brain plays a big role in both classical conditioning and operant conditioning. The obvious example of classical conditioning is Pavlov's dogs, wherein ringing a bell right before feeding them would reinforce that association in the brains of the dogs, so that they would salivate and anticipate food at the sound of a bell even if there was none. In investor terms, this would translate into anticipating financial reward in response to something to some observation, even though the two are not necessarily related and there is nothing to guarantee that a financial reward is forthcoming (this treads a fine line with superstition). Operant conditioning refers to training your brain through reward and punishment. It is a hell of a lot more responsive to reward, though, as animal trainers and child psychologists will note that positive reinforcement is more effective than negative (some going as far as to state that negative reinforcement is completely ineffective, although the research demonstrates otherwise). So, once an investor gets a taste of their first big win, that will trigger a strong neurological response in the brain; but if they lose big, or too frequently, they will either get fired, quit, or in extreme cases they may even commit suicide. At any rate, negative reinforcement tends not to last long in the investing industry, which means the industry is filled with people whose brains are flooded with overactive reward pathways.

The sublenticular extended amygdala is not as clear in the entirety of its functionality, but according to a 2003 study by Liberzon, Phan, Decker, and Taylor, it is proven to be associated with both positive and negative emotional responses to our experiences, stating specifically that, "this region is involved in general emotional processing, such as detection or attribution of salience." As a result, investors experience positive and negative emotional responses which complement the functions of the nucleus accumbens, further reinforcing conditioned responses within the brain.

The ventral tegmental area of the brain is associated with a variety of things, including learning, motivation, and most infamously, with the dopamine pathways in the brain. So, by activating the dopamine neurons in the ventral tegmental area of the brain, investors are flooding their brain with a feel-good chemical that controls things like motivation, sex drive, behavior control, and both reward and reinforcement (which were also associated with the nucleus accumbens). Increasing motivation to repeat the conditioned responses that make them feel good and decreasing their ability to control that behavior results in obsessive, impulsive, and compulsive behaviors which can quickly become erratic and completely irrational.

Finally, the orbitofrontal cortex, while the least understood of the 4 areas of the brain affected in this way, is at least known to be associated with decision-making in response to anticipation of reward or punishment. By activating this region, it further demonstrates that investors are conditioning their own brains to anticipate reward, rather than rationally consider the potential for reward or loss. The result is an increase in risk-taking behaviors and a necessity to continue pushing the limits of risk in anticipation of that reward response. Like in cocaine users, however, many of these processes in the brain (particularly response to increased dopamine levels) does not have the same effect every time – every time we subject ourselves to that stimulus, the effect feels smaller, less potent. So, in order to achieve that same potency that the investor was anticipating, they learn that the next time they must achieve greater rewards, and in attempting to do so they take bigger risks, eventually leading to their own downfall.

This is precisely the sort of behaviors we saw leading into the 2008 financial crisis. Mortgage lenders wanted to achieve higher returns and more revenues, so they began approving borrowers with a much higher risk of defaulting on their loans. Since the risk cost was higher, the lenders charged them higher interest, yet the higher interest rates resulted in higher monthly payments, making the borrowers even more likely to default on their loans, in a loop which I describe as The Paradox of Credit in the book Aspirational Revolution (Taillard, 2017a). This market for high risk mortgages became known as the subprime mortgage market, and the problem had been building for decades. Even as a kid, I remember seeing commercials advertising, "Bad Credit? No Credit? No Problem! All Loans Approved!" Even as a kid, I knew the whole thing was sketchy as hell, so while keeping an eye on that nonsense, in 2007 I tried to tell everyone what was about to happen, but being completely unknown at the time, no one read what I was writing. Finally, in Oct. 2007, the extent of the problem began to become public knowledge, as lenders revealed the true extent of the risks they had taken in pursuit of ever-greater rewards, and that a massive volume of these loans were not going to be repaid. It's a shame really, as the entire thing could have been avoided with just a bit of proper risk management to keep those who were addicted to risk in check.

Anything that gives people a thrill will activate the pleasure centers of the brain, but not in the same way that investing triggers the areas of the brain that control our brain's own ability to reprogram itself and respond more strongly to certain events, limiting out self-control, and causing us to make totally irrational decisions. Once this begins to occur, a person is no longer investing, but they truly are just gambling, and they are doing it with other peoples' money which means they take fewer personal risks in doing so. On the other hand, the application of operant conditioning may explain certain investor behaviors which are seemingly beneficial, if you're willing to suspend all cynicism and think the best of people. There are many managed funds available which are just index funds in disguise. Since index funds outperform managed funds, but managed funds have higher fees and salaries, it makes total sense that a fund manager would be thrilled to perform as well as an index fund while getting paid better for doing it. Yes, I know, this sounds sleazy as hell – the kind of thing only a total shyster would try to pull, taking advantage of people who do are not well-versed in investing to know better. For the moment, we are thinking the best of people, though, remember? If a fund manager is punished for making certain types of investments, then by the rules of operant conditioning, that fund manager would avoid those types of investments in the future. If that same fund manager is rewarded for making certain types of investments, then they will be more likely to make similar investments in the future. It is possible that these managed funds began with a unique portfolio, and over time simply evolve through reward and punishment (gains and losses) to mirror index funds. I choice my wording very carefully, so note that I said it was "possible", and never stated that it was "probable". That is, after all, how conditioning works, but as we already noted in this chapter, investors who experience large or frequent losses tend to leave the industry quite quickly, so the chances that someone would survive a career in investing while incurring losses long enough to create an evolution in their investing style that mirrors an index fund is extremely low.

If the chances of this actually occurring are so low, then you are probably wondering why I even brought it up. Truthfully, it is just a hypothetical scenario that helps demonstrate how malleable our brains are, and how our behaviors respond to external stimuli. It is also a great way to warn people about unscrupulous behaviors among fund managers.

In this chapter alone we have talked about very valid reasons you should not trust investors, lenders, and managers. In the world of finance, is there anyone you can trust? Nope, not in the slightest. In fact, this entire book proves that you cannot even trust yourself, but most people trust themselves more than they trust others. After all, remember that mantra from Chapter 5: "No one cares about my finances as much as I do." That brings us to a classic puzzle in stock markets called the Dividend Puzzle. If you take away behavioral economics and move back to the idea of rational investing, then this would be quite the puzzle, indeed. The Dividend Puzzle states that investors should have no preference for companies which issue dividends or not, yet the reality is that companies which issue dividends tend to outperform on the stock market because investors have a preference for them. The reason it is a puzzle is simple: When a company earns a profit, that money does not belong to the employees, it belongs to the owners, and the owners of corporations are the stockholders. So, those profits can either be given to the stockholders in the form of dividends (just a cash payment), or the profits can be reinvested in the company as something called "retained earnings". Either way, the value of the stock, itself, has not changed. Whether or not investors get cash through dividends, or the value of the company increases through retained earnings, the end result should be the same, leaving the rational investor with no preference.

Returning back to reality, to our insane world containing huge volumes of irrational people all making less than optimal decisions on a constant basis, we find that the reality is that investors really do have a preference – they prefer stocks that issue dividends. Why? It is all about the reward. This is the result of two specific elements which make dividends unique. First, and foremost, is the psychological reward we've talked about all throughout Chapter 6.4. It is that immediate gratification of getting a payout that excites people and activates the reward structures in our brains, giving us a sense of reward that conditions us to prefer dividend-yielding stocks over stocks which do not issue dividends. The second element that makes us prefer dividend-issuing stocks is a bias which I have dubbed the "control bias". Given the option of receiving money and managing it yourself, or letting the executives of a corporation manage it for you, which would you choose? Investors, by their very profession, manage money, and so they would prefer to manage it themselves rather than trust it to someone else. So, they tend to invest in companies which give them greater control over how profits are used. This behavior is then, of course, reinforced, as the person goes and reinvests that money, pursuing that rush once gain. So, not only do dividends give people the immediate gratification reward, but then it also gives them an additional reward by providing them with the opportunity to go through the process again.

Truly, the influence of psychological reward systems in the brain is among the most dangerous things which cause us to act irrationally. This is not just about slight errors or preferences, but it is about a cycle which far too frequently gets completely out of control and can even lead to multinational financial crises. How can you prevent yourself from becoming a psychotic risk-addict? First of all, take a regular inventory of your performance; daily, weekly, whatever. It must be frequent, though, do not think you can get away with 10 year evaluations. State several specific things you did well, and state the exact same number of things you could have done better. Also include several opportunities you found as a result of your actions during that period, and identify an equal number of threats you found during that period. Second, while it is great to get excited over a success, take time to cool-off afterwards and remind yourself that your job is not done yet, and you could just as easily lose your progress if you fail to stay cautious. Above all, remember that people are trusting you to act like a professional, and not a coked-out chimpanzee; would you trust your doctor if they failed to maintain professional decorum? What about your lawyer? How about anyone else you pay? No, of course not, so remind yourself to hold yourself to the same standard of professionalism. Do not just say it, but create an atmosphere of professionalism – a culture within your company or department that highly discourages the use of excess in any way.

6.5 OBSERVATION EFFECT

You are being watched. Followed. Every action you take, every word you say, is being observed, documented, and assessed. There are eyes everywhere, constantly judging your ever move, ever at the ready to respond in retaliation against you in the name of an informal cabal which has conspired against you. You are being watched in real-time as you read this, and all your actions will be publicly available to those who know how to gain access, until the end of time. This is true for the things you do both in the physical world, and in the digital one. There are even two separate sets of standards by which you are being judged, each of them flexible in their interpretation and extreme in their response, making both of them particularly threatening. The more we are aware of it, either by the observers being conspicuous in their own actions or by increasing our awareness of their methods, the more our behaviors change in response to the knowledge that we are being observed. Whether or not you see this as a good or a bad thing does not necessarily depend on your adherence to the standards which are set for your behaviors by the observers, but rather whether you are cognizant that being observed presents as many opportunities as it does threats.

Although the previous paragraph was intentionally written to sound like the rantings of a severely paranoid person, it is entirely true. There are two distinct groups which are watching you, each with their own distinct set of judgments upon which they base their responses to your actions. The first is formal, authorities, which is generally composed of government agencies such as law enforcement, but can also include self-regulatory agencies, companies, and anyone else who is observing you in order to ensure you do not violate laws or policy. Ideally, these laws and policies are clear and consistently enforced in a fair and equal manner. The reality is that they are not. The methods of observation by these groups are more sophisticated, including the use of paid professionals, cameras and satellite imagery, computer and internet monitoring programs, financial transaction monitoring, and more. While these things tend to be monitored in a more timely fashion with old data being largely ignored in storage. The enforcement of these laws and policies tends to involve punitive measures be taken. This may also include foreign governments and spy agencies. The nice thing about authoritative groups like this, though, is that the methods they use are established by policy, making them predictable. For example, several US defense, intelligence, and law enforcement agencies use computer programs that scan emails, social media, blogs, and pretty much everything else in search of specific keywords. These keywords are related to matters of interest to them, so when these keywords appear from a single source in a high enough frequency or concentration that it exceeds a benchmark of statistical significance, the source gets flagged for more thorough review. Well, being fully aware of how these programs worked and the list of words they were searching for, I took several opportunities to use these words on social media in extremely high concentration while talking with other people. While describing to those people exactly what I am describing to you now, I would demonstrate by writing a long list of those keywords, so they were flagged. The reaction of the people in the conversation was, of course, one of panic, until I then took the opportunity to pitch a trilogy of books I wrote on military strategy to whoever would be investigating the conversation. After all, defense and intelligence agents were prime audiences for those books, and what better way to get their attention than by obligating them to read my advertisement to them.

The point of that little anecdote is to demonstrate that observations are not necessarily a bad thing, so long as you find the opportunity to have people observe what you want them to see. In investing, though, what you want people to see is exactly what they want to see: You following every law and regulation to the letter. Investing in the US is primarily observed and enforced in a formal manner by the Securities and Exchange Commission, which was created out of the Securities Act of 1933 and the Securities Exchange Act of 1934. There have since been a lot of refinements to the laws, but the basic ideas behind these laws is that you are not allowed to lie, and you are not allowed to make investing decisions based on information you have privileged access to before that information becomes public (e.g.: if you are a company executive, you cannot trade your own company's stock based on financial information which has not yet been reported to the public). These laws have greatly improved the stock market for everyone. Although there are ways to avoid observation, making investing decisions that violate these laws will always come back to haunt you. These transactions are recorded indefinitely, easily measurable, and unlike little pranks for the sake of advertising a book, the decisions you make in investing will have tangible consequences that will eventually be made known to the public. There is no way to avoid it forever.

The second group watching you is the society around you. They are not so concerned that you follow the law, per se, but if you violate the law then that also tends to violate social taboos. Behaviors which violate the taboos, norms, or other assessments of acceptability will result in informal consequences. What makes social observation so dangerous is that it is extremely fluid, often contradictory, contains frequent disagreements, and has no formal response system in place. So, violating social taboos may result simply in you getting disapproving looks from neighbors, or it may result in a sort-of exile in which you are ignored as a member of society, you may end-up getting harassed or assaulted, or in a worst-case scenario (especially if someone has video documentation of what occurred), the incident can quickly escalate into a judgment of mob rule.

Large groups of people tend to feed on each other's mood, so by the time you have reached the level of "mob rule", it no longer matters what the reality of the situation was, because they just want to see someone severely punished in order to gain a sense of justice and closure, even if it is a total illusion. Observation by society is everywhere. Anywhere you go that there are other people, you are being observed. If you use the internet, or a device with internet connectivity, you can still be easily observed by people exploiting flaws in computer software. This is common among informal social activists like Anonymous, which is a disorganized set of people who self-identify as members, and sometimes find a common things to be angry about, resulting in online harassment. However, as many people have learned, the observed person is also observing others, so when Anonymous tried to attack the Mexican drug cartels, their efforts came to an almost immediate end when it became apparent that one of them was hacked by the cartels, themselves, and their life was put in very serious danger.

Although the actions of investors are often obscure or completely unknown to people who are not familiar with the industry, that does not keep them safe from social responses to inappropriate behavior. In the aftermath of the 2008 Financial Crisis, the CEO of Lehman Brothers (a now extinct investment bank), Dick Fuld, testified before Congress that everyone was at fault for the crisis except him (the reality was that a very large portion of the crisis was his fault). Congress did not prosecute him for his actions, but the very next day while at the gym, Fuld got punched and knocked-out cold by someone who saw the testimony and was clearly not a fan. CNBC reporter Vicki Ward broke the story, and took the side of the attacker, claiming she would have done the same.

Since the threat of reprisal does exist when a person acts like a profound schmuck, whether by law or by being socially ostracized, we tend to change our behaviors when we are being observed. This is called the Observation Effect, and it simply means that when we are aware that we are being observed, we alter our behaviors from what is normal for us in order to stay within the parameters of acceptability within the given context. For example, if you are a financial adviser for fund manager and your customers ask if you participate in insider trading, the answer will clearly be no, because that would be both socially unacceptable as well as illegal. So long as the investor is being closely monitored, they will be forced to avoid any behaviors which would indicate that they are participating in insider trading, but once they are no longer being as closely observed, they will look for ways to violate that law.

Not everything associated with the observation effect is good, mind you. For instance, it makes researchers lives a hell of a lot harder when people do things or say things which they think the researcher (or others in the room) want to hear, rather than what they really want to say. Let me say right now that if you are participating in a research study, just be completely honest and do what comes naturally. There are certain legal and ethical regulations that are put into place when studying human participants that prevent researchers from giving away any information that would identify you. There are even ways to protect that data from a court-mandated warrant. So, help us out – do not be afraid to give us the data we need, rather than the data that you want to give us.

More to the point, though, as an investor, when you are being observed, oftentimes it will change your investing behaviors. For example, depending on the culture of the company you work in, it may be expected that you take greater or lesser risk than you think is optimal given your assessment of the investment portfolio, so you will likely change your behaviors to become what you think is acceptable within that company, resulting in less than optimal outcomes.

There is not much of a way to prevent yourself from doing this on a subtle level, unfortunately. No matter what you do, you will always adapt your behavior at least to some extent depending on who is in the vicinity, or otherwise watching you. What you can do to minimize this impact, though, is to know what you are doing and know exactly why you are doing it. If you can explain your actions and investing behaviors to yourself in a way that based in logic and does not break the law, then you will be better prepared to maintain the behaviors you think are best, regardless of who is watching. The reason, quite simply, is that if you believe you are doing the correct thing, and have the self-awareness to explain it to yourself, then you will be able to explain it confidently to others, leaving you with little reason to change your behaviors. As for those actions which violate the law or social taboos, the best thing you can do is just not do those things, at all. In the financial sector, these things are always revealed, either by an audit, someone noticing inconsistencies, or poor financial reports which come-out later that can be easily traced-back to decisions you made. If you are going to violate laws or taboos, though, then at least be honest about it with researchers. They are only there to collect data and make discoveries about their field of expertise, not investigate criminal cases.

CONCLUSION

So, how is a person supposed to remain calm and logical – tranquil and analytical – all when faced with the chaotic madness that is the stock market? How do you obtain Mr. Spock without becoming Mr. Brooks? The answer just may lie in Buddhism. No, do not worry about all the spirituality stuff. That is not what I am referring to. I am talking about the philosophy of finding tranquility by living purely in the moment and enjoying it for what it is. Eventually we lose everything; wealth, friends, family, health, looks, minds, etc. Everything is temporary, perpetually changing in the impermanence of our very existence. Suffering comes from our own desires, the feeling that we are missing something from our lives which we cannot obtain. The only way, then, to find tranquility, then, is to find it from within. Rather than seeking tranquility, find it from within one's own self, appreciating each moment for what it is rather than seeking what it can never be.

Chapter 7

Mindful Measures

The whole field of behavioral economics spawned from economists' need to better understand the manner in which people make decisions, so we studied the brain to see what causes people to act in ways that makes our jobs harder than they should be. It has been largely ignored, however, that if we stopped using the brain to understand economics, and start using economics to understand the brain, that we can gain important insight into the mental and even physical health of individual people. Economists have been developing a unique variety of very precise measurement and analyses for more than a century, yet it is only now that we are starting to understand how these measurements can be used to read the mind.

So, besides opening opportunities for a new type of fortune telling using bank records instead of palm reading (just call me Monetaro the Mystic), there have been a few critical findings that illustrate that no matter how we try to account for the behavioral oddities we have discussed throughout this book that the stock market will eternally be doomed to be completely irrational. If a perfectly healthy brain functions irrationally, then it would be hypothetically possible to create metrics in trading algorithms which adjust for that. There are more people living in some state of neurological or psychological variation than people realize, though – many people not even recognizing it within themselves. No one is going to claim that the stock market is a place that systematically attracts balanced, mentally healthy individuals; quite to the contrary, the stress of the industry, itself, often leads to mental dysfunction. Not only does our mental state have an influence on our investing activities, but our investing activities have an influence on our mental state. To quote Friedrich Nietzsche, "[...] if you gaze long into an abyss, the abyss also gazes into you." This is a matter which is not so easily incorporated into investing models, unfortunately, leaving the stock market inherently and impossibly irrational for the time being.

So throughout this chapter, we are going to look at the impact of neurological and psychological disorders on the stock market, as well as the role that investing has on our own minds.

7.1 FINANCIAL ABNORMALITIES

Note throughout Chapter 7.1 that I am no longer referring to any of this as "insanity". This particular chapter concerns matters of real neurological or psychological conditions that have a serious and painful impact on the lives of the

Market Insanity. DOI: 10.1016/B978-0-12-813115-2.00007-0

individuals – these people are not insane, they are dealing with any of a number of diseases which affect the brain and have behavioral symptoms. It just so happens that since finance plays such a vital role in our daily lives, and that humanity has spent an eternity perfecting its ability to measure and analyze even miniscule variations in a person's financial behaviors, that when someone is experiencing a malady of the brain, it is often expressed in their finances. In fact, whether or not a person is having financial troubles is typically a consideration when making a diagnosis, though it has yet been overlooked in the medical community that the exact nature of the financial problems being exhibited may be even more useful in diagnosis. To prove this point, let us look at some specific examples, and then we will talk about the broader implications.

As of 2017, the US National Institute on Aging (a division of the National Institute of Health) states that, "Over time, people with Alzheimer's disease lose their capacity to perform the financial tasks of daily living and to manage their financial affairs. In fact, this may be the first noticeable sign of the disease and an early indication that a person is losing the ability to live independently. Research funded in part by the National Institute on Aging (NIA) has shown that Alzheimer's-induced decline in financial skills occurs early and can progress rapidly. Early in the disease process, people with the disease may be able to perform basic tasks such as bill paying or counting change. However, they are likely to have problems with more complicated tasks such as reconciling a checkbook and bank statement, preparing a tax return, or making wise investment decisions. As Alzheimer's disease progresses, all of these abilities gradually are lost, with the more complex skills disappearing first."

Clearly, such complicated financial activities as equities investing will be among the first to demonstrate reduced functionality, meaning that there are a lot of people trying to manage their own investment, or even manage the investments of others, who are not even aware that their ability to make informed investments is being impaired by undiagnosed dementia. It is not until a person is incapable of performing even the most basic financial tasks that their families will tend to insist upon seeing a specialist for diagnosis. Despite that, there appears to be a clear progression in the decline of financial cognition. Work by other researchers have led to the development of tests of generalized cognitive decline in dementia patients using a test of financial activities. For example, work by Al Hazzouri et al. (2014) and others emphasizes the use of tests of a narrow range of financial performance to track cognitive decline in existing Alzheimer's patients. Unfortunately, there is a severe lack of understanding of dementia, and in particular Alzheimer's disease, and there is little useful literature regarding methods for early diagnosis, causation, treatment or intervention, or symptom management. Currently there are roughly 5.5 million Americans currently live with Alzheimer's or dementia, and the ratio of the total population suffering with these conditions is increasing with the demographic shift of the aging baby boomers. According to the World Alzheimer's Report in 2015, the total global cost of dementia is roughly $1 trillion, while dementia care is valued at $818 billion (making it the 18th largest economy in the world, surpassing most nations and corporations). With such a significant impact to the investing markets, it comes as a surprise to many that there has been little or no effort made to identify specific ways to identify dementia-like behaviors among institutional investors before they can have a significant impact.

For proofs-of-concept that financial behaviors can be used to diagnose neurological and psychological disorders, probably no other disease is better-suited than bipolar disorder. Bipolar disorder is a condition in which a person will go through periods of depression followed by periods of manic behavior, typically in a consistent and often predictable cycle. Though not formally used as part of the criteria for predicting bipolar, there are very specific financial behaviors associated with both depressive and manic episodes which are used by clinical psychologists to help the individual. According to the Mayo Clinic, these financial behaviors include: Manic Episode – Increased Spending, Luxury Spending, Increased Investing Risk, Aspirational Pursuits, Increased Debt Volume, Increased Number of Loans, Gift Giving, and Excessive Workloads. Depressive Episode – Late Bill Payments, Unrepaid Debt, Inconsistent Income, Inconsistent Employment, Save-Haven Investing, and Entirely Neglected Accounts.

Given that the financial behaviors symptomatic of a manic episode are so tremendously different than that of a depressive episode, it may be entirely possible to diagnose bipolar strictly by looking at a person's financial data, but clearly it is more professional to use this information is conjunction with other diagnostic criteria. Unfortunately, according to the DSM (Diagnostic and Statistical Manual of Mental Disorders) used by clinical psychologists and psychiatrists, there is little or no concern given to the finer points of financial behaviors.

The reason that bipolar disorder is such a critical disorder for proof-of-concept of the efficacy of using financial behaviors to diagnose neurological conditions in general is that people with bipolar will exhibit not only extreme differences in specific behaviors, but they will typically do so in a cycle predictable by duration of time. People with bipolar will typically cycle through each episode in a consistent period of days, weeks, or months; which would correlate perfectly with their financial behaviors. Should the volatility of investment risk aversion, just as a possible example, be a reliable indicator of a guaranteed diagnosis of bipolar, then all the subjective, qualitative diagnostic criteria is unnecessary, leaving no room for errors. The diagnosis would simply be one of exceeding a statistical threshold of volatility in one's financial behavior.

Even more significantly, this provides interesting opportunities to improve treatments. For example, if an individual with bipolar disorder is taking a particular medication and the degree of financial volatility they exhibit reduces, then the accuracy and reliability with which the benefits of that medication can be measured increase dramatically compared to qualitative observational analysis and patients self-reporting their symptoms. This holds great potential in the realm of research for treatments of neurological diseases, but for the pur-

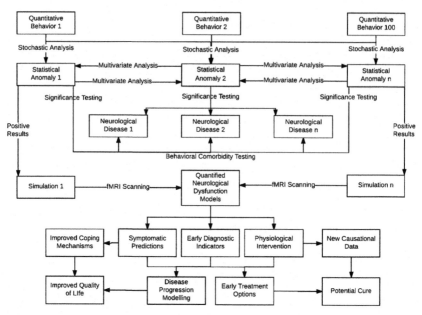

FIGURE 7.1 Behavioral Economic Model for Neurological Research

poses of this book the more important factor is that it improves the ability of an individual to predict and improve their investing behaviors. By being able to accurately calculate the exact financial impact their episodes have on their investing behavior, and predict when these episodes will occur, there is no reason that the individual should not be able to incorporate a very reliable stochastic adjustment to their strategies, even going so far as to program such an adjustment into a computer algorithm to automatically adjust their investing activities and correct for the deviation from rationality caused by their condition. With a bit more sophistication, an algorithm could be programmed to identify when an episode is occurring, and take actions to correct errors, or to prevent certain types of transactions. Roughly 5.7 million Americans live with bipolar disorder, the vast majority of them doing their best to manage their finances, including investments and retirement accounts, yet people wonder about the irrationality of the stock market and whether it can ever be improved. The answer, as far as we know so far, is yes.

This exact same research data and methodology can be used as a way to identify statistical thresholds of financial volatility for a wide variety of neurological and psychological conditions, making it useful as a diagnostic tool and as a tool to evaluate the efficacy of various treatment options for patients in a clinical setting by measuring changes in volatility over time. This methodology also offer a unique opportunity to identify the functions of the brain and model it with great precision. It all comes-down to what you see in Fig. 7.1.

Each person's financial behavior is going to be unique, so it does not do very much good to begin by simply comparing irrationality between people, because even completely healthy people manage their investments in an irrational manner, as we have seen throughout this book. So, it has to start a little slower, by looking deeply into the financial behavior of individuals over time. If a person at some point in their lives is diagnosed with a neurological condition, you start by looking deeply at that person's behaviors over the course of years. There is a huge volume of potential behaviors which one could assess, just a small sample of which includes:

Spending Behaviors – Total value of spending, Types of goods purchased, Frequency of purchases, Medium of payment used, etc.

Income Behaviors – Consistency of income, Variety of income sources, Distribution or use of income, Levels of disposable and discretionary income, etc.

Risk – Credit score, Liquidity and solvency, Gambling habits, Investment portfolio risk metrics, Asset management, etc.

Debt – Types of debt, Total value of debt, Number of individual loans, Defaults, Debt ratios measured against income and liquidity, Interest rates being paid, Sources of debt such as banks or payday lenders or family members, etc.

Billing – Number and frequency of later payments or payments which are missed entirely, Duplicate payments accidentally made, Accuracy in paying at least the minimum amount owed, consistency in the amount paid each period, etc.

Banking/Brokerage – Transaction volume, Performance metrics in brokerage accounts, Risk cost incurred, Frequency and severity of banking errors made, etc.

Taxation – Accuracy of tax filings, Consistency of deductions and credits, Frequency and value of tax penalties, etc.

Anomalies – Lost endowment effect, Deviations from expectations, Altered anchors, etc.

The list goes on and on, but by the off-chance that this book gets some notice, I want to keep the majority of the metrics, particularly the more obscure ones, proprietary. Academic publishers do not pay enough for me to reveal everything, after all.

At any rate, within all these different behavioral variables you are looking for statistically significant levels of volatility, deviations from what is normal for that person, any unusual autocorrelative patterns, and things of that nature. It may be a single variable, or there may be some interplay between variables, so a bit of understanding of how to program automated data analysis would be beneficial during this process. If a person with a neurological condition does exhibit financial behaviors which are odd for that particular individual leading-up to their diagnosis and afterward, then it comes time to compare that particular oddity with other people that have the same mental malady. If that odd behavior is consistent between everyone who has been diagnosed with the same condition, then you really know you are onto something big. It is at that point it becomes possible to perform diagnosis and treatment efficacy testing using the financial behaviors in question, as described in the earlier conversation about bipolar disorder.

There is already a theoretical basis for this, starting in the 1970s when Kahneman and Tversky identified consistently anomalous behaviors in risk decisions based on the presentation of information. In surveys, identical scenarios presented to study participants yielded different responses based on presentation, and even a small degree of uncertainty produced a disproportionately large degree of aversion. This proved for the first time that the presentation of information actually matters more than the information being presented when making decisions of risk and reward. Since then, this has been confirmed in a wide variety of studied related specifically to the financial sectors. Behavioral variables, and behavioral cluster analysis, have been demonstrated to be strongly correlated with financial decisions such as those associated with earnings management (Callen, Morel, & Richardson, 2011), dividend management (Shao, Kwok, & Guedhami, 2010; Guedhami et al., 2010), capital risk management (Baik et al., 2012), social financial performance, (Ho, Wang, & Vitell, 2012), and equity investment risk aversion (Taillard, 2017b). The problem is that, although financial behaviors are shown to have a great degree of potential in helping us to better understand a diverse set of neurological factors, the literature heavily emphasizes the use of neurology and psychology to improve financial performance, almost entirely ignoring the potential for financial behaviors to provide insight into neurological functionality. Financial behaviors have been entirely overlooked both as an indicator or marker of neurological function, and greatly ignored as a focus of symptomatic intervention.

This approach is even more profound, however, than simply being able to diagnose, help treat, and improve the lives of people with neurological and psychological conditions, however. Given the vast significance that such progress may have not only for the field of medicine but also for improving the financial sector by limiting the influence of these mental conditions on investing decisions, it may be difficult to believe that there is something even more significant that could come from this data. This was proven, though, in 2005 by Gonzalez et al., when they recreated the experiments performed by Kahneman and Tversky during the 1970s, but this time while placing participants under an fMRI (a bit machine that takes a sort-of video recording of your brain activity). By doing this they identified a neurological basis for the phenomenon first recorded some 30 years before. Specific neurological functions were consistently identified and analyzed, as seen in Fig. 7.2.

The table you see lists a variety of different areas of the brain, then measures whether each responded in a way that was statistically significant while making decisions about risk and reward scenarios. It came as no surprise that the frontal and parietal lobes were activated, as these are the areas of the brain wherein we

Sum of the change signal intensity (SSI) per ROI and condition

ROI					Frame	Risk	Frame × Risk	Risk in positively framed problems E
	Positive/certain	Positive/risky	Negative/certain	Negative/risky	$F(1,9)$	$F(1,9)$	$F(1,9)$	$F(1,9)$
Frontal								
LDLPFC	11.7	16.8	18.9	17.4	n.s.	n.s.	n.s.	n.s.
LFEF	7.9	12.6	13.0	15.8	n.s.	n.s.	n.s.	n.s.
LOPER	6.3	7.3	8.2	7.4	n.s.	n.s.	n.s.	n.s.
LPOSTPRECEN	4.7	9.9	8.0	9.4	n.s.	n.s.	n.s.	n.s.
LTRIA	1.7	1.8	1.0	1.9	n.s.	n.s.	n.s.	n.s.
RDLPFC	12.5	29.4	18.8	22.9	n.s.	3.8*	n.s.	7.2**
RFEF	5.5	11.3	4.6	5.0	n.s.	n.s.	n.s.	n.s.
ROPER	0.7	2.5	2.9	1.1	n.s.	n.s.	n.s.	n.s.
RPOSTPRECEN	3.7	7.7	5.2	4.0	n.s.	n.s.	3.9*	6.23**
RTRIA	0.5	2.5	1.3	1.2	n.s.	n.s.	n.s.	n.s.
SMA	4.4	4.7	5.3	5.8	n.s.	n.s.	n.s.	n.s.
SMFP	12.6	17.6	21.3	18.6	n.s.	n.s.	n.s.	n.s.
Sum	**72.0**	**124.1**	**108.6**	**110.5**	n.s.	3.41*	n.s.	n.s.
Parietal								
LIPL	8.5	16.4	16.0	13.1	n.s.	n.s.	5.4**	4.51*
LIPS	18.4	38.7	28.1	32.7	n.s.	4.88*	4.0*	8.71**
LSGA	0.3	2.5	1.3	0.6	n.s.	n.s.	n.s.	n.s.
LSPL	5.2	9.5	6.7	5.4	n.s.	n.s.	n.s.	n.s.
RIPL	8.9	13.3	13.7	10.1	n.s.	n.s.	n.s.	n.s.
RIPS	30.7	53.6	40.8	41.4	n.s.	8.88**	n.s.	15.69***
RSGA	0.0	0.7	0.5	0.4	n.s.	n.s.	n.s.	n.s.
RSPL	10.8	21.8	13.3	13.6	n.s.	n.s.	n.s.	6.61**
Sum	**82.9**	**156.5**	**120.5**	**117.2**	n.s.	3.96*	n.s.	10.60*
Temporal								
LIT	3.3	4.0	7.0	4.7	n.s.	n.s.	n.s.	n.s.
LT	0.9	2.1	3.9	2.9	n.s.	n.s.	n.s.	n.s.
RIT	6.0	4.9	8.6	4.5	n.s.	n.s.	n.s.	n.s.
RT	0.6	1.0	4.6	1.1	n.s.	n.s.	n.s.	n.s.
Sum	10.7	12.0	24.1	13.2	n.s.	n.s.	n.s.	n.s.
Occipital								
CALC	19.0	27.2	28.2	29.0	n.s.	n.s.	n.s.	n.s.
LIES	31.6	40.7	36.1	38.1	n.s.	n.s.	n.s.	4.38*
LSES	5.7	5.9	3.6	3.6	3.99*	n.s.	n.s.	n.s.
OP	38.1	51.3	46.7	39.2	n.s.	n.s.	n.s.	n.s.
RIES	17.4	32.7	23.6	19.4	n.s.	n.s.	3.7*	6.77**
RSES	6.1	7.0	5.0	8.5	n.s.	n.s.	n.s.	n.s.
Sum	117.7	164.9	143.2	137.7	n.s.	n.s.	n.s.	n.s.

* $p < 0.05$.
** $p < 0.01$.
*** $p < 0.001$.

FIGURE 7.2 Neurological Response of Risky Decisions

make decisions, and process information, respectively. It was significant enough for the purposes of the study to simply prove that there was a neurological basis for the anomalous behaviors identified by Kahneman and Tversky, and that they were, in fact, able to specifically identify which parts of the brain were associated with assessments of risk or assessments of reward. The authors of the 2005 study understated the implications of their findings, however. Not only did they fail to mention to potential for these findings to create the foundations upon which research into neurological disorders could be assessed using detailed financial analyses, but they failed to report on the fact that participants in the study had their occipital lobes activated when assessing potential rewards, but not potential risk. This activation of LIES and RIES in assessing reward potential, yet not risk aversion, indicates previously unknown function of occipital lobe, which is typically associated only with vision-related functions, such as hand-eye coordination. This unusual finding implies that there is the potential for financial analyses to actually develop detailed models of how the brain functions by simulating a wide range of financial decisions and activities, discovering totally unknown physiology.

That is where the bottom half of Fig. 7.1 comes into play. Once a specific investing behavior has been identified as being definitely associated with a specific mental disorder, then it becomes possible to scan the brain activity of people with that disorder, as well as people who do not have that disorder, while participating in simulations of that particular investment activity. Using a control group of "healthy" individuals is necessary in order to determine whether the variations in brain activity in the study group are consistent, otherwise there would be no way of knowing what is the baseline for normal brain function in these investing activities. The results of these scans, ideally, will illustrate exactly what areas of the brain are being activated by specific types of investment activities, while also identifying the physiological cause of the disorder in question, allowing us to improve our understanding of how to prevent, treat, or even cure some disorders, if not at least disrupt their progression. If nothing else, it will most definitely help us to provide people suffering from mental conditions with better coping mechanisms, so that they can make better financial decisions, and manage their investment portfolios more effectively. As stated before, these coping mechanisms could come in the form of simple self-awareness, or in the form of predictable algorithmic adjustments to the calculations and transactions being made.

So, when we are talking about common neurological diseases such as Parkinson's Disease, with which more than 10 million people around the world cope, having predictive models of the financial impact of such a condition would be extremely beneficial. In 2013, Santangelo et al. performed a meta-study which showed a strong association between the onset of Parkinson's disease and an increase in risky behavior, most prominently pathological gambling. Those being treated with any drug of the dopamine agonist class are particularly susceptible to such increases in risky behavior, as the data showed these individuals experienced a downregulation of frontostriatal connections and dysfunction of fronto-subcortical circuits which could be to blame. This would be consistent with the research performed by Gonzalez, Dana, Koshino, and Just (2005), which demonstrated the frontal lobe was most strongly associated with assessment of risk when making decisions, and studies subsequent to Gonzalez demonstrating a strong and consistent correlation between financial risk aversion and those behaviors associated with the neurological functions identified in risk aversion as implied by research published by Taillard in 2017. So clearly, in terms of investment risk, this is a matter of great concern given the number of people who are diagnosed with Parkinson's. Thankfully, however, the probability and degree of decreased risk aversion is measurable and predictable, allowing investors with Parkinson's to incorporate a simple mathematical adjustment to their valuation projections, making their investing decisions more rational than would otherwise be possible for them.

As a final note on mental disorders and their impact on investment, it has been shown that psychopathy is much more prevalent among stock market investors than the general population. According to studies by Canadian forensic psychologist Robert Hare, there population-at-large contains roughly 1% of people with psychopathy, while in the financial services industry that rate jumps to 10%. This might be triggering memories of Huey Lewis and Christian Bale in a poncho, playing-out Bret Easton Ellis' novel American Psycho. That is not the type of psychopath we are talking about. Psychopathy is not a condition of all-or-nothing; there are degrees of severity, and even high-functioning psychopaths. A fantastic 2012 article in CFA Magazine by Sheree Decovney describes the impact of psychopathy on investors in detail, providing prominent examples of known psychopaths in the financial services industry. She states that, "Taken to the extreme, some traders become compulsive gamblers. The behavior is often latent—neither they nor anyone else knows they have this propensity. They hide small losses and keep doubling their position to try to eliminate them. When those trades turn sour, they dig themselves into a deeper hole and deny any wrongdoing or failure. They rationalize by telling themselves that poor investment decisions are an occupational hazard. They lie to family members or others to conceal the extent of their involvement with gambling and commit forgery, fraud, theft, and embezzlement to support their habit." Since psychopaths lack empathy or interest in what other people think or feel, these activities do not phase them in the slightest, nor do other activities we've discussed in this book, such as financial advisers selling products or making transactions which harm their clients because it benefits them personally. It is difficult to say what the exact impact of this is, and according to Wall Street psychologist Christopher Bayer, the rate of psychopaths is higher than 10%, but even that is difficult to confirm because in high functioning psychopaths, the exact traits that can make them harmful are also the traits that make for ideal investor, fund manager, CEO, etc. According to Bayer, "[They] generally lack empathy and interest in what other people feel or think. At the same time, they display an abundance of charm, charisma, intelligence, credentials, an unparalleled capacity for lying, fabrication, and manipulation, and a drive for thrill seeking." This is exactly the type of person who can make decisions without being emotionally phased by them (as demonstrated to be bad in Chapter 6), and, if properly managed, may even be able to engage the stock market without their investing decisions being influenced by emotion. It does seem that there is a fine line, however, in that the negative traits of psychopathy tends to produce situations such as that associated with people like Kweku Adoboli, Jerome Kerviel, and Nick Leeson; each of whom lost billions of dollars for their companies, and their clients, with their unscrupulous behavior.

7.2 BUYING HAPPINESS

Looking at Chapter 7.1, we discussed the impact of neurological abnormalities on investing behavior and what can be done about it, but as previously noted, the investment markets themselves tend to take a mental toll on people actually causing them to develop psychological disorders. Most frequently, these are related to extremely high levels of stress or anxiety, although the environment is one that also tends to induce narcissistic and/or sociopathic tendencies within individuals who may have a higher predisposition toward pathological behaviors of this nature. In any case, the world of professional or otherwise full-time investors tends to have a high labor turnover rate, meaning that it attracts a lot of people because of the high earnings potential but that most of those people tend to have careers which are shorter than most other industries because of the psychological toll it takes on them. These mental issues are predictable, but often have an unpredictable impact on each individual. By far the most common mental disorders which occur among investors are stress-related. This does not just result from the working environment of the financial sector, because it happens to independent full-time investors, too; but rather, it results purely from the nature of being obligated to have money properly invested as a full-time objective.

To quote a short passage from another of my books, "Money cannot buy happiness, but it can resolve many of those things which cause us distress. It can eliminate the possibility of homelessness by paying-off a mortgage, it can ensure we have access to proper healthcare, it can allow us to feed our children, and much more. So many people, their ultimate financial goal is simply to be without any major threats to their health and relationships." In 2010, Deaton and Kahneman did a study which conclude that a person in the US must earn $ 75,000 per year to avoid unhappiness resulting from financial insecurity. The exact same conclusion was made in a different study performed in 2016, after accounting for inflation between 2010 and 2016, by Clingingsmith which confirmed that as a person's income increases, their level of unhappiness rapidly decreased until the point that they are earning $80,000 annually.

Unfortunately, those who are professional investors or who invest independently full-time do not have the luxury of reaching a point of "good enough" (see Chapter 4 for the discussion on Satisficing behavior) – a state in which financial risk is no longer a concern. To the contrary, managing financial risk successfully is a constant concern, and one upon which their careers depend. Even private investors have a degree of luxury in avoiding the tremendous mental strain that professional investors experience, because they are not obligated to be constantly invested in the market. Famous investor Ben Graham, apparently having a few loose screws, himself, used to anthropomorphize the stock market (that is the fancy way of saying he would treat the stock market as a person, talking about it in terms of human traits). He would say that Mr. Market will make an offer at any moment, and if that offer is not to your liking you can always say "no". He saw this as a luxury because Mr. Market would always come back the next day with a new offer, leaving the independent investors like Warrant Buffett with a great degree of freedom. Professional investors, by contrast, must have all the assets under their management invested in some manner. They have been left in charge of other peoples' money, and do not have the luxury of saying "no" to Mr. Market, but if a particular investment option is not favorable then the professional investor must have an alternative investment available. Simply holding onto someone's cash without investing it is not an option. So, professional investors experience the constant pressure of financial risk not only as an inherent part of their job, but if they fail in their role then their own financial status will be put at risk, as well. To compound the problem, investment managers and brokers will very often have clients who are neurotically-obsessed pests who will contact them multiple times in a single day to get status updates, so that there is always someone looking over the shoulder of the professional investors, breathing down their neck in critical judgment of every single investment, lack of investment, or delay in investment made. Needless to say, the pressure can be overwhelming.

The effects that this has on the stock market and our investing decisions varies widely, however. High levels of stress can cause a person to take unnecessarily high risks in an aggressive and desperate attempt to generate returns that results in an investment portfolio that crashes, or it could cause them to become too afraid to take any risk at all, resulting in a stable portfolio that underperforms. High levels of stress can lead to panic attacks, in which a person simply breaks-down and cannot function in a professional capacity at all until the attack subsides. Stress can also cause people to leave the profession entirely, and often people are relieved to have found a different career path.

Instead of making casual claims on this matter, let us look at some real research. According to the US National Institute of Health, stress causes a wide variety of physical and neurological complications. As of 2017, their official statement is that, "Health problems can occur if the stress response goes on for too long or becomes chronic, such as when the source of stress is constant [. . .]. [. . .] chronic stress, [. . .] can suppress immune, digestive, sleep, and reproductive systems, which may cause them to stop working normally. Different people may feel stress in different ways. For example, some people experience mainly digestive symptoms, while others may have headaches, sleeplessness, sadness, anger or irritability. People under chronic stress are prone to more frequent and severe viral infections, such as the flu or common cold.

Routine stress may be the hardest type of stress to notice at first. Because the source of stress tends to be more constant than in cases of acute or traumatic stress, the body gets no clear signal to return to normal functioning. Over time, continued strain on your body from routine stress may contribute to serious health problems, such as heart disease, high blood pressure, diabetes, and other illnesses, as well as mental disorders like depression or anxiety."

It is important to note in the previous passage the statement which addresses the extraordinary problematic issues surrounding routine stress. This type of stress is the kin that does not result from any sudden and temporary trauma, but rather from a constantly ongoing source, such as that found in a high-stress career. It is this type of stress which becomes habitual, wherein a person becomes accustomed to a degree of stress but since the source of the problem persists the stress levels in the individual can continue to rise. According to the US National Library of Medicine, uncontrolled stress, in extreme cases, can even lead to brief psychotic episodes, in which a person may become delusional, have hallucinations, exhibit unusual speech or language, and otherwise act abnormal for an otherwise healthy person. Unfortunately, this type of extreme reaction does not have predictable effects on a person's investing decisions, although it will be much more readily noticeable so that an intervention can be taken before it has any long-lasting impact on an investment portfolio.

As previous mentioned, the investing profession tends to inherently cause narcissistic and sociopathic tendencies within people who previously did not exhibit such behaviors. This may result from human tendency to conform to the social atmosphere in which they exist, or it may result from a neurological feedback loop during the sales process (in other words, people need to appear entirely confident and competent to acquire clients, and by falsely presenting that appearance early in one's career they eventually fall for their own bullshit), or perhaps these careers simply attract people with a higher predisposition for such behavioral problems and that the constant application of self-serving bias (discussed in Chapter 3) gives them an outlet through which to expand their narcissistic behaviors. Maybe it is a combination of factors which contributes to this, but there is most certainly a distinct culture of alpha-personality dominance which permeates the realm of professional investors which inevitably swallows nearly everyone who enters the field. This, of course, has implications for the nearly-omnipresent overconfidence, misperceived risk, self-serving bias, and a number of other irrational behaviors already discussed throughout this book.

To put this all simply, investing has a negative impact on a person's mental health, and a person's mental health has negative consequences for their investing decisions, the failures of which magnify the impact that investing has on their mental health, and so forth in a cycle that leads investors and bankers to have a slightly higher rate of suicide than the national average. This is not just a trend of Wall Street during the start of a recession, either; it is a trend that occurs just as much in other major financial sectors such as London and Hong Kong, as it does in New York; and trends of suicides tend to remain particularly elevated in the years leading up to a recession, and the years following one.

So, what can investors do to prevent their own careers from driving them stark raving mad, resulting in clearly irrational behaviors associated with investment decisions? Unfortunately, as of this very moment, not much. There are a wide variety of methods available to manage stress and anxiety, and even to maintain independent, rational thought in a chaotic atmosphere. However, professional investing careers are very competitive and extremely results-oriented. If you do not perform, then you are considered extremely expendable. So, although you might be able to find a proper work/life balance, take time to enjoy nature, socialize with family, or pursue a hobby, in your career you are constantly being exposed to operant conditioning via means of extreme rewards and extreme punishment by the very structure of the industry. There is little room for a tranquil individual seeking rationality in an industry dominated by a culture of workaholics obsessed with miniscule comparisons of your performance against others in the industry. All you can do is try your best to ignore the hyper-competitive atmosphere and explore different was to manage your stress. No, consuming large volumes of alcohol and drugs (legal or otherwise) are not healthy ways to deal with stress, either, so get that out of your head right now.

7.3   MONEY, MARRIAGE, AND FAMILY

The relationship between money and our personal relationships seems to be one of those things that is hard to pin-down, initially, but is entirely obvious once it has been explained. As the old saying goes, "Hindsight is 20/20". Once the impact of our investing behaviors has on our family relations becomes clear, then a wide number of implications become possible.

Lots of people like to think that when they get married and start a family, that money was not a factor in their decision. They like to think that their decision was because there was a perfect match, or it was about true love, or some other poetic nonsense. Especially among Western nations, there is an insistence that marriage is about finding that "perfect someone", and that you will be together "for richer or for poorer." Well, there is some bad news and there is some good news.

First the bad news. According to a study done by Divorce Magazine in 2013, "Financial Troubles" was the #1 cause of diverse in the US. During that same year, the Institute for Divorce Financial Analysts performed a study stating "Money Issues" was the #3 cited reason for divorce. Just a year later, a study was released by the Austin Institute for the Study of Family and Culture citing "Financial Priorities" as the #6 cause of divorce. In the last of these studies, other reasons cited include things like "spousal immaturity" and other explanations which are so broad that they are likely to include irresponsible financial behaviors, so it seems probable that financial matters actually play a greater role than expressed using that particular survey.

Looking at these surveys, one might be forgiven for assuming that vowing to stay with your spouse through times of "poorer" is a bad bet. It would appear that when times get rough financially, it breaks families apart just for the simple fact that being poor sucks, and that it inherently causes a strain on our personal relations. So, if you are an investor, you might be tempted to avoid marriage altogether, or if you have a family then it is quite likely that you feel an additional sense of obligation and responsibility to not jack-up your investment portfolio. This perception, alone, can play a role in our investing performance. If someone believes that the performance of their investment portfolio is inherently tied to the success of their marriage, then that will most definitely have strong implications for the degree of risk aversion a person has, assuming they value their marriage (in fact, let us go ahead and just assume for the rest of this chapter that we are talking about people who actually want to be married for reasons other than being a gold-digger). If someone goes into an investing profession and convinces themselves that either their marriage or their career or both would be doomed due to the ties between finances and personal relationships, then they may very well end-up with intimacy issues that leave them no meaningful connections, which is not healthy. People go mad in solitary confinement, and self-imposed confinement is far more difficult to recognize.

Thankfully, it is not as simple as all that. Prior to those casual pop-surveys, a legitimate study was performed by Dew et al. in 2012, which states that, "When financial disagreements were in the model, financial well-being was not associated with divorce. Both wives' and husbands' financial disagreements were the strongest disagreement types to predict divorce. These findings suggest that financial disagreements are stronger predictors of divorce relative to other common marital disagreements." These findings also suggest that it is not the absolute financial well-being of a family that causes divorce, but rather differences in opinions between spouses regarding the manner in which the finances should be managed. Ok, granted, it is a lot easier to get into fights over money when you do not have much of it. Simply, when there is not enough money to meet everyone's needs, then there are going to be disagreements about how best to allocate the available funds. So, yeah, being poor will increase your chances for divorce, but not necessarily so, as long as both people in the marriage are financially compatible.

Yeah, we are going to go full-on Cosmo Magazine now and talk "Is your boyfriend marriage material? Find out by looking at his investments!" Again, we are assuming that we are talking about people who want to get married, not people who are in it just for the money. So, the point here is that, according to the research, one of the best predictors of whether or not a relationship will work-out is whether you have the same financial goals, priorities, and habits. If money trouble is one of the top reasons people get divorced, and that trouble is the result of disagreements about money rather than the amount you have, then getting married to someone who is financially compatible should logically reduce your chances of divorce by a tremendous percentage. Of course, there are not any studies done to prove that, as of yet, so this is all mere logical inference. It would be a fun study to perform, though, so after this book comes-out, I suspect there will be someone out there who jumps on the opportunity.

Think about it for a minute: Theoretically, we could come-up with an index that measures the likelihood that a couple will get divorced even before they get married. By using the same approach as Edward Altman in developing his infamous "Altman's Z-Score" (apparently he was better in finance that he was giving names to things), it is likely that such a thing would not only be possible, but quite accurate. If you are not familiar with Altman's Z-Score, it is a mathematical model that predicts whether a corporation will file for bankruptcy within 1 year, with roughly 90% accuracy. The equation is as follows:

$$Z = 1.2x_1 + 1.4x_2 + 3.3x + 3 + 0.6x_4 + 0.999x_5$$

It is a very simple weighted financial model wherein:

$x_1 = $ Working capital divided by total assets

$x_2 = $ Retained earnings divided by total assets

$x_3 = $ Earnings before interest and taxes divided by total assets

$x_4 = $ Market value of equity divided by total liabilities

$x_5 = $ Sales divided by total assets

If Z is less than 1.81, than the company is most certainly going to file bankruptcy within the next year, while if Z is greater than 2.99 there is almost no chance at all of an impending bankruptcy. Between 1.81 and 2.99 lies the zone of uncertainty, though clearly the closer the value is to 1.81 the more likely a company is to file bankruptcy.

Using this same approach and applying it to the personal financial behaviors of individuals, it would be possible to calculate with great accuracy the degree to which the financial behaviors between them differ. That would provide an indicator of whether or not they will have disagreements over financial matters, which could theoretically be an accurate prediction of whether or not a marriage will work-out. If nothing else, it would make for a great feature article in some pop-culture magazine.

It is time to finally get to the point of all this, though. The influence that marriage and family has on your financial decisions goes well beyond simple matters of tax filings and budgetary concerns, and it even goes well beyond the potential for an added sense of obligation which can contribute to the stress a person feels both about their finances and their marriage, resulting in increasingly irrational financial decisions (as discussed earlier in this chapter). Your own investing behaviors will be directly influenced by the goals, priorities, and behaviors of your spouse. There is a degree of compromise which must occur for any household to remain functional, and one of the most prominent issues to arise, as already addressed, is the matter of finances. So, getting married and attempting to maintain a healthy relationship will influence your investing decisions based on the financial behaviors of your spouse. The degree to which this occurs depends greatly on how similar the financial behaviors are between spouses – if they are already very similar before getting married then things will not change very much, while if there was a great degree of difference then there must either be a great degree of change or else a total dissolution of the marriage (i.e.: divorce). As an investor, rather than avoiding relationships altogether, you can predict what kind of changes will occur to your investing behaviors after getting married by assessing the financial behaviors of your spouse. The same can be said for married people who are simply managing their finances; it is possible to improve the performance on your investment portfolio by comparing each person's financial performance and favoring the person with the better financial background. That does not mean giving total control of the finances to one person or the other, as such dramatic changes are the kind which end in divorce. Instead, take a more refined approach and adjust financial decisions in favor of the person with better financial performance by a ratio equivalent to the difference in performance. That way, there is provided a valid balance between improving finances while saving an otherwise viable relationship.

CONCLUSION

Yeah, this chapter delved heavily into the speculative, the theoretical, and the truly unusual. You were warned from the very start of this book, though, that our minds function in bizarre ways, often actively working against us in our attempts to remain sane and rational. To my knowledge, there is not a single person in the history of the entire planet that has successfully accomplished this feat, so naturally the content of this book will necessarily, at times, reflect the insanity that lies within the wrinkly little fold of our brains. I always do like saving the most speculative topics for last, not only because it prevents people from getting scared-off in the first chapters, but because it is those proven and well-studied behaviors which lay a solid foundation upon which we realize the speculative has merit. Throughout this chapter the one thing that is not speculative in the slightest is that each of these matters do influence our investing decisions, and that there are ways in which we can account for that. Whether or not our investing decisions can be effectively used to improve our state of mind still requires more research. Just get in touch with Elsevier if you want to offer me any grant money to research these topics. They will know how to get in touch with me.

Conclusion

Well, that's the book. Between all the problems in our ideas, and behaviors, and emotions, and even our perception, it can most definitely be said that investing is all in the mind of the individual. Some might try to argue that even though the individual person is not rational, that the stock markets average-out to something that is either efficient or rational or both. As we have shown in this book, that is all balderdash, or maybe even poppycock. Either way, it is wrong. The collective sum dumb decisions simply does not make for an optimal outcome, unless you live in a movie being made by Mel Brooks. The truth is that we are each behaving poorly in our own unique ways, and though there are many common traits we all share, the distinct signature of any person's loony brain can be seen on the history of any investment portfolio.

Your financial behavior even has tell-tale signs of where you were born and/or grew-up. This is done using something called cultural dimensions, which are spectrums of specific types of behavior that vary between cultures. For example, "uncertainty avoidance" is a dimension of culture that is shared among several different cultural researchers, and it refers to the degree to which (as you may have guessed) the people of a nation avoid uncertainty. Low uncertainty avoidance means people are more comfortable with accepting things as they are, are not as concerned about strict plans or regimens, and so forth. People with high uncertainty avoidance feel the need to be certain of everything, planning everything to the tiniest detail, and not straying from what is expected. There several different competing sets of cultural dimensions, and all of them only really work when you look at a nation or cultural region as a whole. The more you try to apply these dimensions to localities, subcultures, or even individual people, the less reliable these cultural dimensions are (a problem called the "ecological fallacy"). Even so, these cultural dimensions can be seen in the stock markets, and the way in which people respond to the stock market is telling of where they live.

Shao, Kwok, and Guedhami (2010) were able to conclusively demonstrate that the value and frequency of dividends being paid by corporations is significantly related to the cultural dimensions of Mastery and Conservatism. These particular dimensions of culture were developed by Shalom Schwartz at the Israel Social Sciences Data Center in 1994. Shao and his buddies went out to explore the mysteries of the dividend puzzle, (you know, the one we talked about in Chapter 6.4), and instead of discovering anything related to what they were looking for, instead they found that dividend policy, itself, results greatly from the influence of culture on the same perception issues we discussed in Chapter 5. More conservatism means more frequent and higher value dividend payouts, while more Mastery does the exact opposite. Conservatism and mastery refer to the tendency of a nation's people to maintain modesty and self-control, and their tendency to seek individual success apart from the society in which they live, respectively.

In another study, Callen, Morel, and Richardson (2011) went in search of whether or not culture plays a role in earnings management. If you're thinking that "earnings management" is a bit broad a term to really pin-down, you would be correct. So, they used an index of earnings management that was developed by Christian Leutz at the University of Pennsylvania business school. Earnings management may sound like a good thing, but it really is not, as the factors included in this index include the use of accrual alteration to reduce volatility in reported earnings, the use of accrual alteration to reduce volatility in reported operating cash flows, use of accounting discretion to mitigate the reporting of small losses, and the use of accounting discretion when reporting operating earnings. In other words, "earnings management" refers the how much people fudge their financial reporting, rather than how well the reinvest their earnings. Callen's team found this sketchy behavior to be associated more strongly in nations with high levels of uncertainty avoidance and with low levels of individualism. Both of these dimensions were taken from the cultural dimensions developed by Geert Hofstede. We already talked about uncertainty avoidance, but individualism is the degree to which people see themselves as distinct from their society, while the opposite of individualism is called collectivism, and refers to cultures in which people tend to see themselves as a part of a larger society.

Hofstede's original work only involve 4 dimensions of culture, of which two have already been described here in the Conclusion. The other two are power distance, and masculinity vs. femininity. Yeah, before we get to the matter of bizarre nomenclature, first let us describe power distance. Power distance is the amount of height in the hierarchy – it is the degree to which your overlords are seen as superior and your minions are seen as inferior. Lower power distance would refer to a culture in which people are seen as relatively equal, which is hardly conducive to supervillainy. The successful supervillains exist in a culture of high power distance, so that orders are obeyed without question and dissidents can be crushed with an iron fist (or whatever other type of fist you happen to have handy). As for the "masculinity and femininity" cultural dimension, I have no explanation for the name. Even in academic research, people make note that these labels are curious at best, and an expression of the male-dominated global patriarchy that seeks to suppress the rights and freedoms of women at its worst (no one has actually made that kind of an accusation in a research paper, or any other paper, to my knowledge; but they were thinking it awfully loud). Whatever the reason for it, "masculine" nations are those who tend to favor individual success, the pursuits of power and wealth, and competition. "Feminine" nations are those which tend to favor social cooperation, the pursuit of health and happiness, and a more egalitarian society. Come to your own conclusions about the names, but what we know for sure is that all 4 of Hofstede's dimensions were significantly correlated with corporate social performance.

Corporate social performance is one of those things that investors care about but cannot decide amongst themselves whether it is a good thing or a bad thing. Simply, it refers to the tendency for companies to be concerned with benefitting all the people that the company's operations effect, rather than just the shareholders. The private financial management firm Innovest and evaluates 120 corporate performance factors from four categories: stakeholder capital, human capital, strategic governance, and environment. Some people say that this makes a company more valuable and competitive, other people say that this represents a non-value added cost that should be direct back into company growth. In 2012, when Ho Et Al (which is a really common last name in citations; are all these Et Als related?) wanted to know whether or not culture played a role in the tendency of companies to allocate resources to social performance, the team used the Innovest index are analyzed data collected compared to Hofstede's original cultural dimensions. What they found was that higher amounts of power distance, masculinity, and uncertainty avoidance increased corporate social performance, but higher amounts of individualism decreased it. The conclusion we can draw from this is that when people have the authority and drive to ensure that a company is working toward the best interest of everyone, then it will happen so long as the person given that authority is not a self-serving jerk (or responsible steward to the shareholders, depending on how you view it).

The investors, themselves, respond to all this in different ways, as well. Like we already discussed at the end of Chapter 3 on the matter of "home bias", increasing access to global capital markets have given investors way more opportunity both to increase their returns by finding better investments, and diversify-away the chance that the entire economy in one's own nation will go down into the gutter. Instead of doing any of that, though, they decide to ignore foreign investments, possibly because they end-up having to pay a premium for those foreign investments. From where does this cost premium come from? Differences in perception between the investors of different nations, of course. Xu, Hu, and Fan (2009) demonstrated that greater differences between cultures actually plays a role, decreasing the amount of investments made between those countries, while nations which are more culturally similar invest between each other more greatly. This was later confirmed in 2012 by a team led by Baik which proved that both cultural differences between nations as well as the amount of unfamiliarity investors have with a given culture both reduce the degree to which investors are prone to invest in the stock market of any particular country. Baik's team also confirmed that cultural differences and being unfamiliar with a foreign culture hurts the future returns you make in the stock market of that nation. This is where we find that a cultural cost premium exists for foreign investments. The obvious conclusion is that people are completely misunderstanding what is happening in the minds of investors with different cultures than their own, and as a result their calculations of value and risk are all wrong when applied to foreign investments.

Still, global equity markets continue to integrate, though. The two largest factors on that integration are the proportion of gross domestic product which is composed of investments between two nations, and the proportion of total trade for each of those nations that is composed of trade with each other. In other words, the more business that nations do together, the more their stock markets become integrated. Both of these things, themselves, are driven by behavioral sources emphasizing the amount of difference in the cultures of two nations. The UN World Investment Report in 2013 showed that regional economic integration is occurring at a more rapid rate than distant foreign integration. This confirmed a study by Kivilcim and Muradoglu (2001) which illustrated that nations which are geographically near to each other have more integrated equities markets, while the study of cultural dimensions by Robert House showed that there are distinct cultural regions which are grouped together geographically. Since bigger differences in culture between nations reduces the amount of investment between those nations, the cultural differentials will be more prominent in nations which are very distant, leading to a curvilinear relationship wherein differences in investing behavior changes at an faster rate with greater degrees of cultural distance. This was proven by yours truly in 2017 when in a study wherein I used the overlapping cultural dimensions of Geert Hofstede and Robert House to prove that the degree of loss aversion among investors in a given nation was largely determined by cultural factors. The results of this study remained constant not only over a 20 year period but using two separate methods of measuring cultural dimensions, and the data definitively showed a moderate curvature to the relationship between cultural factors and investor loss aversion.

Where you are from also determines which factors are useful in developing stock valuation calculations. In Jordan, a study found that 84% of volatility in stock returns could be explained by incorporating money supply, interest rate term structure, industry productivity growth, and risk premium into the valuation models; but neither inflation rates nor dividend yield were of any use, at all. In Nigeria, value and risk models were improved by including both real gross domestic product as well as the consumer price index, but trying to find a use for foreign exchange rates was an utter waste of time. In Zimbabwe, only money supply and oil prices were found to be useful predictors of stock market valuations, and the study could find nothing else that was helpful. India found a bunch of useful factors that were useful in developing valuation and risk models, including exchange rate, wholesale price index, gold prices, and market index. A supposedly comprehensive global study by some people out of Romania attempted to identify if any factors of stock market valuation were globally universal. They claim to have identified interest rates, inflation, and industrial production, as being useful factors in every nation, although this does contradict other studies mentioned. The Romanian study also found that exchange rate, currency exchange volume, and trade were all unique to Romania, although this, too, contradicts other studies.

When simple geography determines absolutely so much about how investors behave, calculate value and risk, and how they perceive and respond to even common metrics of value and risk, it becomes obvious that there is no one, single "correct" answer to whether an action is rational or not. Even if one investor generates greater returns, an investor of equal experience and skill may perceive those returns as being insufficient to warrant the amount of risk that was incurred in the process. Hell, that disagreement happens all the time even within a single office building, much less on a global scale, so there is absolutely no hope for finding a truly "rational" answer, because what is rational is nothing more than a construct we develop for ourselves to help us make sense out of the world around us. The stock market is all in the mind, though, and everyone's mind is a little bit different, with its own unique fingerprint of insanity.

That being said, there is a massive difference between the short-run and long-run fluctuations in the stock market. Although the insanity we have discussed throughout this book lasts indefinitely, ceaselessly driving us to self-destructive ends, but that does not mean investors are completely oblivious. When things get far too extreme – when the continued irrationality of our decisions bring us to a point at which we can no longer justify or rationalize its ongoing persistence, there comes something called a "correction". For example, in regards to herd behavior, investors may drive the market price of a specific stock up well beyond its actual value, but eventually it will dawn on those investors that what they are doing is utterly insane; that the current market price is nowhere near what is expected. The result is that the price comes crashing back down again. You see, the thing which defines "short-run" and "long-run" in economics is somewhat different than you may be familiar with. If you are into accounting or finance, then short-run is defined by any time period shorter than 1 year, and the long-run is anything exceeding a year. If you come from a psychological background, then these terms are more subjective, and can refer to a range of circumstances. In economics, and consequently in financial economic assessments of the stock market, the distinction between short-term and long-term is defined by the longest period of time required to adapt to changes in the market. In other words, in the short-run, investors will not be able to fully adapt to changes in the conditions of the stock market (primarily as a result of the things discussed in this book), but in the long-run investors can adapt to anything. To illustrate this concept, imagine a company that makes sweaters for camels using an automated knitting machine, when the consumers realizes that their camels do not particularly have any need for sweaters. Most likely, this company will spend the most time altering its machine to produce sweaters for a different market (in this case, for alpacas). So, the period of time necessary for this company to adapt to changes in market conditions will be equivalent to the time necessary to modify their knitting machine. Since alpacas are not so differently shaped than camels, the company can accomplish this in 60 days. Thus, the short-run for this company is any time period shorter than 60 days, because they would need more time to adapt to changes in the market. The long-run would be anything greater than 60 days because then they could adapt to any change in the market. In the stock market, the long-run tends to be quite a bit longer, though, frequently spanning a period of multiple years. Still, as the market conditions change and investors finally come to realize that they need to adapt to their newly found perception of the market, things will invariably change back towards something which more closely resembles rationality.

That is the problem with stock market – we only come to understand would have worked best in hindsight, and even when looking upon the past there are disagreements. If you were given an opportunity to invest in Microsoft when it first began operations, you absolutely would, but only because you already know how that story ends. At the time, however, it would have been seen as an extremely risky venture, and most people turned them down. It was only in the long-run, when it dawned on people that they missed a big opportunity that the investment markets really began to take notice, and the market price of Microsoft quickly escalated to something more closely aligned with the current value of their future earnings. So, much of what we have discussed in this book is related to the short-run, while in the long-run markets tend to have greater degrees of rationality. That is not to say that investors ever come to their senses – no, far from it – even the long-run is composed of nothing more than a never-ending string of sequential and parallel short-runs. What this does imply, however, is that as you expand the time horizon on an analysis, the analysis will come to resemble something closer to rationality. If you sit there and watch the daily chaos of the markets, what you are seeing is 100% pure madness, but if you look at trends in the market over the course of a 1, 3, or 5 years, then things start to look more stable. Of course, the cruel taunting hidden within that fact is that the longer your time horizon is, the less useful the data will be. Investment data about a company that is from 20 years ago will be practically useless, except to the most sophisticated analysts and researchers; and even for them, the vast majority of what they would need to do could be accomplished with 10 years of data or fewer, making 20 years unnecessarily burdensome and costly.

It is true that the introduction of the behavioral paradigm to investing complicated matters quite quickly. Everything that was once held a sacred seemed to crumble and fall between the fingers of history. What seemed like a simple matter of better understanding of rational investing ended-up being something far more unpredictable and harder to assess, oftentimes with no singularly correct answer, and markets were clearly shown to be far from the efficient medium for the distribution of capital resources that people once imagined. There is still good news for those who remain in denial about these matter, though. As mentioned several times throughout the book, the factors that contribute to the insanity can be treated in an identical manner to the rational factors you know and love. They can be studied, measured, analyzed, predicted, and incorporated into models of arbitrage pricing theory just like anything else. You just have to come to understand a bit of psychology first, instead of merely assuming that people act rationally. The discoveries behind the behavioral paradigm, though, bring us a large step closer to finally understanding the stock market in its full glory, and answers many of the questions which previously seemed impossible to resolve. As a result, humanity is just that much closer to achieving the ideal circumstance of the stock market: maximized economic growth and efficiency of resource utilization through the optimal distribution of capital assets to sources that produce the greatest value of outputs using the fewest volume of inputs. As strange as it may seem, even to investors, understanding the stock market in this way – as a medium for capital allocations – brings into perspective the importance of its role to maintaining sustainable resource management with an ever-growing population.

The future of investing is going to get extremely interesting and take-off in directions no one could have ever guessed. We are beginning to find ways to predict the future by identifying leading indicators into the decisions people will make and how many people will make certain decisions. There is research occurring right now that utilizes search trends on Google or other search engines to determine what search terms are significantly related to specific investment decisions, so that it is possible to estimate what people are actually considering doing in a serious enough manner that they would research the possibility first. We will continue to better understand ourselves and others in order to improve the returns on our investments, that is obvious, but this will also provide important insight into the psychology and neurology of people, as well. As described in Chapter 7, I am currently developing models to improve diagnostics and treatment efficacy of mental conditions so that we can identify these conditions sooner, help people cope with them more effectively, and possibly even identify new methods of treatments and cures. Unfortunately, as it stand, the fields of economics and medicine are entirely separate, with no applied overlap to speak of, making it extremely difficult for economists to interact with patient data and interpret the physiological results of medical tests, and extremely difficult for doctors to acquire and understand data on financial behaviors. Although the barriers on this matter are strong today, in the future we will see a much stronger degree of interdisciplinary study which provides us with the opportunity to finally develop a comprehensive understanding of what makes people do the things they do. As finance and economics has expanded to psychology, and in the future to neurology, we will finally come to understand ourselves, and perhaps even put an end to the insanity.

Afterword

Computer technology lets us do some really cool stuff. We can explore the universe, cure the sick, communicate with anyone instantaneously, and even completely clobber the entire stock market from a home computer in less time than it takes to make microwave popcorn. Our technology is integrated into our homes, our businesses, our government, and even our very living bodies – wearables that augment our perception of the reality around us, and wireless implants like pacemakers that keep us alive (yes, they can be hacked). Yes, thanks to convenience and efficiency that is the modern computer, we have integrated every aspect of our lives, and can automate any aspect of our daily routine, including the management of our investment portfolios. The real question, though, is whether or not they have allowed us to improve our financial management, instead of just speeding it up and automating it.

In a way computers have improved our financial management. It is a standard feature of online stock trading platforms that we should be able to place buy or sell orders in advance, including a variety of different transactions that are only carried-out under specific conditions, otherwise the brokerage firms do not charge a dime. Setting orders at specific prices, or volumes, or times, have all allowed for a variety of very interesting and advanced strategies, but nothing compared to what can be performed when programming your own platform through which orders can be directly placed through a brokerage firm (or if you are a broker, you can execute these trades directly). There are no limits to the types of orders we can pre-program – grey areas which do not exist in the simple packages, transactions which are only executed after a complex calculation has been solved by a given market price, transactions which occur in response to other transactions in order to maintain a specific degree of risk on the overall portfolio, and so much more.

More importantly, we can program not just transactions, but perform groundbreaking research and develop new analytical and valuation models based upon that research which is entirely proprietary – secret from the public for use to our own advantage. Not that keeping advances in research and analytics a secret is inherently the point, although it can be very lucrative for those of us with a talent for quantitative finance, but it is the research and analysis that not only improves our strategies, but they improve our fundamental understanding of how the stock market functions. Advancing our knowledge of the underlying factors which drive capital allocations and market valuations, and the manner in which these factors can be incorporated into complementary equations, is vital to improving both the returns on our own investment profiles but also the efficiency with which we utilize limited global resources to stimulate growth and improve the quality of life for people around the world. Do not worry, I am not going to start preaching about the environment and stuff like I am Captain Planet, but it is important to note that improvements to our understanding of global capital markets does, in fact, do more than develop wealth – it improves our ability to utilize the resources available to us in the best possible manner; growing the volume of wealth available and, ideally, the manner in which we utilize that wealth. In a world that measures every transaction using currency, quantitative financial analysis is the method by which we calculate the ideal utilization of global capital.

The reason that computers have made such research possible is that they have allowed us to perform calculations and analyses using large data sets that would have been otherwise unreasonable to perform by hand, and that means developing new tools to improve our financial decisions. Not only does having more data to test a single hypothesis improve the accuracy of your analysis, but have huge sets of data on a wide variety of factors allows us to test for significant relationships between those factors by automating the process – programming a computer to repeat specific series of analytics and statistical tests an impossibly large number of times can help to uncover important factors or relationships which otherwise would not have been noticed. This is a process called data mining, and while it is nice for sorting through huge data sets, it only identifies trends in the data without defining the exact reason the trend exists. It is at that point that individual researchers look at the trends and perform thorough research on it, confirming the results and placing them within the context of the already-existing literature and theoretical constructs on the topic. In other words, data mining is a bit like cold calling, while research closes the sale. Once we understand how the new information fits together, it can be incorporated properly into equations that predict future market values, the degree of risk involved, the improvements to a change in strategy, and so forth. Unfortunately, despite all this cold, mechanized analysis, we still incorporate our own neuroses not only into the decisions we make using the latest equations, but into the equations, themselves. The goal of reaching anything even close to rational decision-making is a long way off yet, so more times than not we are actually using the latest computer technology to facilitate our own insanity. We are using these incredible technological advancements to make our madness more potent in the market.

Everything discussed in the Afterword is accomplished through the development and application of something called an algorithm. Really, that is just a fancy way to refer to a set of instructions to be performed when given the signal to do so. For example, the flowchart that was included in Chapter 7 and

Fig. 7.1 was, in fact, a visual illustration of an algorithm; it tells you what to do at each step in the process, and how to make decisions based on the outcome of certain tasks included in a given step. Eventually you get to the end of the algorithm, and the instructions have all been completed. This is the manner in which computers are programmed to automate tasks – through algorithms.

Most online trading services allow you to establish some simple algorithms. You can set a variety of orders in advance which are only executed if they meet certain conditions. For example, you may want to use a limit order to purchase some stocks if it can be purchased at a particular price or better, and a stop order which will sell stocks if the market price drops below the purchase price. These are all very common types of stock orders, but by making them in advance you are giving the computer an instruction to follow some directions you've given it. That is the basis of an algorithm. People will use a variety of different buy and sell strategies to make money, and as a person continues to give the computer additional instructions to execute additional types of orders in sequence, the algorithm that is being programmed becomes more complex. Most traders and investors do not even realize they are building algorithms in this way, because they are simply choosing from a small menu of available order types they can make and placing them, but for the computer, each of these orders represents a very specific set of instructions, and when these are sequenced together to form a trading strategy, then the final outcome of the algorithm is the value of your investment portfolio.

Once you start talking about institutional investors – particularly those who emphasize quantitative finance – things start to go way beyond the basics, as they hire people to program more sophisticated proprietary algorithms, wherein trades are triggered based on a customized analyses of several factors, going as far as to include a risk analysis of the total investment portfolio and trade stocks based on predetermined parameters of statistically-calculated risk. It is possible to include streaming data into an algorithm, so that it is constantly calculating changes in the equations developed based on whatever you want, whether you are getting the data from common sources like Bloomberg Terminal, unorthodox sources like Google search trends, or even developing your own streaming data by programming bots to screen news headlines and analyze the frequency and distribution of specific keywords which may appear.

Sounds pretty complicated, huh? It can be, but we are not worried about building algorithms in this book, we are worried about the insanity. The point is simply that with our ability to automate our investment transactions based on premeditated plans, and our ability to program objective analytics right into the algorithms which perform our trades, the impact of our own mental weirdness should be mitigated, right? Think again! Not only are we programming our computers to automate our neurological irrationalities, playing-out bizarre decisions so quickly that it would look like a total psychological breakdown if performed by an individual instead of a computer, but the use of computers has actually allowed us to invent brand new types of insanity.

First we will take a quick look at how we program insanity. As discussed in Chapter 6, even using computer automation, our own neuroses are still permeated directly into the program. Every instruction that is included in the algorithm you give a computer is a decision that you must make. The computer will not create its own instructions, no matter how advanced it is, or even if you are using artificial intelligence. Even artificial intelligence is merely a set of instructions given to a computer which allows the computer to automatically adapt to changes in the data it receives. For example, when you get shopping recommendations from online stores, or viewing suggestions from streaming video services, that is a very basic form of artificial intelligence – the simplest form of machine learning. It functions by collecting data on what people buy or watch and starts making associations. If a single person watches a particular movie, and then watches another movie, then the artificial intelligence will make a weak association. If lots of people watch those same two movies, then the artificial intelligence will increase the statistical significance of their being a correlation between those two movies. So, when you finally go and watch one of those movies, the artificial intelligence will be able to recommend the other based on a statistical analysis of the data. So, while you could develop an artificial intelligence algorithm that starts with a base trading strategy or valuation model and automatically adapts to changes in market prices or financial metrics, the manner in which it adapts to these things (as well as the things to which it responds) are all determined by you and the instructions you provide.

Since even the most advanced algorithms are based on instructions provided an individual, the same insanity that the individual would exhibit when making investments on their own will still shine through like a ray of sunshine on a cloudy day in the algorithm they build. As a result, their computer-automated investing activities are just as neurotic as they are. If a person has a particularly strong home bias, then they will program their algorithm in such a way that they do not even assess foreign investment options. If a person is prone to herd behavior, they will program the algorithm to take into consideration significant movements in the market, perhaps even including a simple moving average that would cause exaggerated future valuations during a market upswing. The most common and more omnipresent things in these algorithms, though, is our propensity for behaviors based on a person's psychological frame. The orders we place, even when placed in advance or programmed to be placed, demonstrate the same perception of risk and degree of risk aversion, the same assessment methods of potential gains, the same timing of trades being executed (though perhaps more quickly and efficiently), and the same prospect theory-based behavioral phenomena that were discussed all throughout Chapter 5. Computers only do what we tell them to do, and we only tell them to do what we want them to do, and in the world of investing, what we want does not change just because it is being done by a computer. Quite to the contrary, one of the things that makes artificial intelligence in the stock market so tricky is that since it includes our own insanity, unless you are very careful in the instructions you provide, the artificial intelligence could easily end-up adapting in a way that exaggerates our insanity to an even greater degree than we would exhibit it, ourselves. Like a funhouse mirror, the artificial intelligence could become a distorted reflection of ourselves, making outrageous investment decisions.

Instead, let us imagine that you have developed a perfectly rational trading algorithm. Most automated investing does not get so involved to become monstrosities with the potential to become self-aware and intentionally manipulate the stock market in a bumbling attempt to destroy humanity, nor are they ever fully rational. Instead, most typically, they are just about as insane as the rest of us. So, just for the sake of argument, let us imagine that you have stumbled upon a way to automate your stock investments in a manner that is perfectly rational thanks to some new algorithm you developed. Good for you, but you are still not out of trouble yet. Even the most rational of investing strategies, incorporating tools to help account for our own irrationality, have become a problem thanks to computers. Since such a huge percentage of the total stock market trades are being performed by automated algorithms these days, it has actually resulted in the integration of otherwise totally separate systems, from different institutional investing firms, each with their own irrational behaviors. The instructions you give your computer may result in an investment that triggers another computer halfway around the world to make a different investment, creating a globally-connected system of disconnected systems. In a way, we have created a worldwide algorithm that is so completely mad in every way that it would result with someone being put into prison. Come to think of it, that has actually happened!

This new form of market insanity possible only as a result of the interaction between computers is best illustrated by something called a "flash crash". A flash crash occurs when multiple investors have their automated trading strategies set-up in just the right way to create a perfect storm, causing an entire market to drop up to 99% of its entire value for just a very short period. A great example of this happened on June 22, 2017 with the cryptocurrency Ethereum (cryptocurrencies are kind of like real money, except that they are almost completely useless). The investment was trading at $317.81 until a single sale dropped the market price just enough that it triggered everyone else's computers to execute a stop-loss order, which means everyone's computers began selling Ethereum because the price had dropped to the point that people were afraid it would drop even further – they did not want to incur any additional losses (hence, calling it a "stop-loss order"). In just 45 milliseconds, the price of Ethereum dropped to $0.10, losing 99.999% of its total value. That's roughly the frame rate of a single frame of film when you are watching a movie – you will see 24 frames of film every second of a movie and it looks seamless, so 45 millisecond is so fast that your brain could not process drop fast enough to actually see it happen. Of course, everyone had already programmed their computers to buy Ethereum if it dropped below a certain price, so it only took 10 seconds from the price of Ethereum to rush back up to $300, just 5.9% lower than it had originally started. All this financial drama that would have caused a global panic had it been any slower, broke out and then resolved itself again before anyone knew what had happened.

Of course, whenever people are not paying attention to their own behaviors, there will be a person there to take advantage of them. This was the cause of the 2010 Flash Crash, which was the first major flash crash to occur, and drew the attention of law enforcement, regulatory agencies, computer security experts, financial experts, academic researchers, and eventually led to actions being taken in the US federal government to identify the cause and try to develop ways to prevent it from happening again. An entire 5 years later, the US Department of Justice arrested a person named Navinder Singh Sarao, a London-based trader, although it is hotly debated whether he was the real cause or whether he was a convenient scapegoat because he was participating in some illegal market manipulation (the question is whether or not his actions could have caused the flash crash). Currently in prison, the accusation was that he used an automated program to trick traders in a method called "spoofing", which involved placing thousands of sell orders of E-mini S&P 500 stock index futures contracts, worth roughly $200 million, which were altered over 19,000 times before he finally canceled all of them. He called the order "cancel if close", in which the orders were canceled if the market price got close the sale price. This drove the drove the US stock market down by roughly $1 trillion in just 5 minutes. The happened because he knew that the vast majority of investment transactions were automated, and that the vast majority of the algorithms use by traders took into consideration the price of futures contracts. So, by putting huge volumes of futures up for sale, it caused traders to automatically sell stocks, driving down the market price, at which point Sarao would cancel the sale of the futures contract and buy-up stocks cheaply. So bold was this tactic that the futures exchange actually contacted him the same day of the flash crash, just before it happened, to tell him to stop, to which he responded, "Kiss my ass." He allegedly made $40 million in profit from the crash.

The problem with the idea that Sarao, alone, could have caused the 2010 crash on his own is that he was not arrested until 2015, and the Department of Justice claims he continued this behavior for several subsequent years. Since spoofing is such an obvious behavior with such severe consequences, this would have resulted in several more flash crashes between 2010 and 2015. The prevailing theory is that Sarao's actions, in combination with existing negative investor sentiment resulting from Greece's financial woes, triggered a stop-loss order in the algorithm used by the asset management company Waddle and Reed. Whether Sarao was responsible on his own for manipulating algorithms, or he simply contributed to a flash crash that was likely to occur anyway as a result of cascading stop-loss orders, it all comes back to the behaviors we program into our own computers to automate our financial transactions. In any case, it wouldn't be a flash crash if there was no recovery, and in 2010 it took only 20 minutes for the US markets to recovery roughly the entirety of their value.

Technology is awesome! It is getting better, too. Right now there is a Canadian company called D-Wave which is the first company to sell functioning quantum computers. That is to say, they utilize quantum entanglement so that the computer can process computations in parallel rather than linearly (this is where I tell you not to ask too many questions, because this stuff gets complicated really fast, and belongs in a book on quantum physics rather than finance). The point is that a quantum computer can run more than 100 million times faster than today's high-end consumer computers. Of course, with all the potential that this has to do amazing things for humanity, what is it that D-Wave chooses to include in their marketing? The stock market! While yes, that is true, the markets could theoretically use a quantum computer, as we have already discussed, it will only increase speed, not quality. The markets function only as efficiently as our ability to develop quality algorithms, and not even a quantum computer needs people to tell it what to do, so it seems as though our insanity will very soon become "spooky". (That last line refers to Einstein calling quantum entanglement "spooky action at a distance".)

Bibliography

Akerlof, G. A., & Kranton, R. E. (2011). *Identity economics: How our identities shape our work, wages, and well-being*. Princeton, NJ: Princeton University Press.

Akerlof, G. A., & Shiller, R. J. (2009). *Animal spirits: cómo influye la psicología humana en la economía*. Barcelona: Gestioón.

Armstrong, W. J., Knif, J., Kolari, J. W., & Pynnönen, S. (2012). Exchange risk and universal returns: A test of international arbitrage pricing theory. *Pacific-Basin Finance Journal, 20*(1), 24–40.

Baik, B., Kang, J., Kim, J., & Lee, J. (2012). The liability of foreignness in international equity investments: Evidence from the US stock market. *Journal of International Business Studies, 43*, 107–122.

Basu, D., & Chawla, D. (2012). An empirical test of the arbitrage pricing theory—The case of Indian stock market. *Global Business Review, 13*(3), 421–432.

Beugelsdijk, S., Maseland, R., & Hoorn, A. V. (2015). Are scores on Hofstede's dimensions of national culture stable over time? A generational cohort analysis. *Global Strategy Journal, 5*(3), 223–240.

Bodie, Z., Kane, A., & Marcus, A. J. (2013). *Investments* (10th ed.). Boston: McGraw-Hill/Irwin.

Brakman, S., Garretsen, H., & Marrewijk, C. V. (2006). *An introduction to geographical economics: Trade, location and growth*. Cambridge: Univ. Press.

Callen, J. L., Morel, M., & Richardson, G. (2011). Do culture and religion mitigate earnings management? Evidence from a cross-country analysis. *International Journal of Disclosure and Governance, 8*(2), 103–121.

Camerer, C. (1997). Progress in behavioral game theory. *Journal of Economic Perspectives, 11*(4).

Chen, M., Lakshminarayanan, V., & Santos, L. (2006). How basic are behavioral biases? Evidence from capuchin monkey trading behavior. *Journal of Political Economy, 114*(3), 517–537. http://dx.doi.org/10.1086/503550.

Christelis, D., & Georgarakos, D. (2013). Investing at home and abroad: Different costs, different people? *Journal of Banking and Finance, 37*, 2069–2086.

Clingingsmith, D. (2016). Negative emotions, income, and welfare: Causal estimates from the PSID. *Journal of Economic Behavior & Organization, 130*, 1–19. http://dx.doi.org/10.1016/j.jebo.2016.07.004.

Cohn, A., Engelmann, J., Fehr, E., & Marrchal, M. (2015). Evidence for countercyclical risk aversion: An experiment with financial professionals. *American Economic Review, 105*(2), 860–885.

Dixon, H. D. (2001). Some thoughts on economic theory and artificial intelligence. *Surfing Economics*, 161–176. http://dx.doi.org/10.1007/978-1-137-04142-5_7.

Eiteman, D. K., Stonehill, A. I., & Moffett, M. H. (2013). *Multinational business finance* (13th ed.). Boston, MA: Pearson/Addison-Wesley.

Field, A. (2013). *Discovering statistics using IBM SPSS statistics, vol. 4* (4th ed.). SAGE Publications.

Geambaşu, C., Jianu, I., Herteliu, C., & Geambaşu, L. (2014). Macroeconomic influence on Shares' return study case: Arbitrage Pricing Theory (APT) applied on Bucharest Stock Exchange. *Economic Computation and Economic Cybernetics Studies and Research, 48*(2), 133–150.

GLOBE (2012). College of Business. Retrieved October 15, 2012, from http://business.nmsu.edu/programs-centers/globe/instruments/.

Gonzalez, C., Dana, J., Koshino, H., & Just, M. (2005). The framing effect and risky decisions: Examining cognitive functions with fMRI. *Journal of Economic Psychology, 26*, 1–20.

Grenness, T. (2012). Hofstede revisited: Is making the ecological fallacy when using Hofstede's instrument on individual behavior really unavoidable? *International Journal of Business and Management, 7*(7), 75–84.

Gul, A., & Khan, N. (2013). An application of arbitrage pricing theory on KSE-100 index; A study from Pakistan (2000–2005). *Journal of Business and Management, 7*(6), 78–84.

Hinton, B. L. (1968). An empirical investigation of the Herzberg methodology and two-factor theory. *Organizational Behavior and Human Performance, 3*(3), 286–309. http://dx.doi.org/10.1016/0030-5073(68)90011-1.

Ho, F. N., Wang, H. D., & Vitell, S. J. (2012). A global analysis of corporate social performance: The effects of cultural and geographic environments. *Journal of Business Ethics, 107*(4), 423–433.

House, R. (2013). *Strategic leadership across cultures: The GLOBE study of CEO leadership behavior and effectiveness in 24 countries* (1st ed.). SAGE Publications.

Isenmila, P. A., & Erah, D. O. (2012). Share prices and macroeconomic factors: A test of the arbitrage pricing theory (APT) in the Nigerian stock market. *European Journal of Business and Management, 4*(15), 66–76.

Jecheche, P. (2012). *An empirical investigation of arbitrage pricing theory: A case Zimbabwe.*

Kagel, J. H., Battalio, R. C., & Green, L. (2007). *Economic choice theory: An experimental analysis of animal behavior.* Cambridge: Cambridge University Press.

Kahneman, D. (2006). *Would you be happier if you were richer?: A focusing illusion.* Princeton, NJ: Center for Economic Policy Studies, Princeton University.

Kahneman, D. (2015). *Thinking, fast and slow.* New York: Farrar, Straus and Giroux.

Kahneman, D., & Deaton, A. (2010). High income improves evaluation of life but not emotional well-being. *Proceedings of the National Academy of Sciences, 107*(38), 16489–16493. http://dx.doi.org/10.1073/pnas.1011492107.

Kahneman, D., & Tversky, A. (1981). *On the study of statistical intuitions.* Ft. Belvoir: Defense Technical Information Center.

Kahneman, D., & Tversky, A. (2009). *Choices, values, and frames.* New York: Russell Sage Foundation.

Kivilcim, M., & Muradoglu, G. (2001). Forecasting integrated stock markets using international comovements. *Russian and East European Finance and Trade, 37*(5), 45–63.

Lopez, A. C., Mcdermott, R., & Petersen, M. B. (2011). States in mind: Evolution, coalitional psychology, and international politics. *International Security, 36*(2), 48–83. http://dx.doi.org/10.1162/isec_a_00056.

Lopez De Leon, F., & Renata, R. (2014). A test for the rational ignorance hypothesis: Evidence from a natural experiment in Brazil. *American Economic Journal: Economic Policy, 6*(4), 380–398.

Machina, M. (2014). Ambiguity aversion with three or more outcomes. *American Economic Review, 104*(12), 3814–3840.

Madan, D. B. (2014). Asset pricing theory for two price economies. *Annals of Finance*, 1–35.

Members (2015). Key Information. Retrieved December 4, 2015, from http://www.world-exchanges.org/home/index.php/members/wfe-members.

Merkle, C., & Weber, M. (2014). Do investors put their money where their mouth is? Stock market expectations and investing behavior. *Journal of Banking and Finance, 46*, 372–386. Print.

Minkov, M., & Hofstede, G. (2012). Hofstede's fifth dimension: New evidence from the world values survey. *Journal of Cross-Cultural Psychology, 43*(1), 3–14.

Myagkov, M., & Plott, C. R. (1994). *Exchange economies and loss exposure: Experiments exploring prospect theory and competitive equilibria in market environments.* Pasadena: Cit.

Oswald, A., Proto, E., & Sgroi, D. (2015). Happiness and productivity. *Journal of Labor Economics*, *33*(4).

Pollison, M., & Renou, L. (2016). *Afriat's theorem and Samuelson's 'Eternal darkness'*. University of Leicester.

Preis, T., Moat, H., & Stanley, H. (2013). Quantifying trading behavior in financial markets using Google trends. *Scientific Reports*, 1684.

Prince, M. (2015). *World Alzheimer report 2015: The global impact of dementia: An analysis of prevalence, incidence, cost and trends*. London: Alzheimers Disease International.

Quinlan, C. (2011). *Business research methods*. Andover, Hampshire, UK: South-Western Cengage Learning.

Ramadan, I. Z. (2012). The validity of the arbitrage pricing theory in the Jordanian stock market. *International Journal of Economics and Finance*, *4*(5), 177.

Roberts, S. C. (2012). *Applied evolutionary psychology*. Oxford: Oxford University Press.

Rubinstein, A. (2002). *Modeling bounded rationality*. Cambridge, Mass: MIT Press.

Samuelson, P. A. (1938). A note on the pure theory of consumers behaviour: An addendum. *Economica*, *5*(19), 353. http://dx.doi.org/10.2307/2548634.

Sarapultsev, A., & Sarapultsev, P. (2014). Novelty, stress, and biological roots in human market behavior. *Behavioral Sciences*, *4*(1), 53–69. http://dx.doi.org/10.3390/bs4010053.

Saunders, A., & Cornett, M. M. (2013). *Financial institutions management: A risk management approach* (8th ed.). Boston: McGraw-Hill/Irwin.

Shao, L., Kwok, C. C., & Guedhami, O. (2010). National culture and dividend policy. *Journal of International Business Studies*, *41*(8), 1391–1414.

Shi, X., & Wang, J. (2011). Interpreting Hofstede model and GLOBE model: Which way to go for cross-cultural research. *International Journal of Business and Management*, *6*(5), 93–99.

Shi, J., Bilson, C., Powell, J., & Wigg, J. (2010). Foreign direct investment and international stock market integration. *Australian Journal of Management*, *35*(3), 265.

Shiller, R. (1979). Can the Fed control real interest rates? https://doi.org/10.3386/w0348.

Shiller, R. (1980). Do stock prices move too much to be justified by subsequent changes in dividends? https://doi.org/10.3386/w0456.

Shiller, R. J. (1981). *The use of volatility measures in assessing market efficiency*. Cambridge, MA: National Bureau of Economic Research.

Shiller, R. J. (1989). *Initial public offerings: Investor behaviour and underpricing*. Cambridge: NBER.

Shiller, R. J. (2007). *Understanding recent trends in house prices and home ownership*. Cambridge, MA: National Bureau of Economic Research.

Shiller, R. J., & Shiller, R. J. (2016). *Irrational exuberance*. Princeton: Princeton University Press.

Siddiqui, S. (2012). Business bankruptcy prediction models: A significant study of the Altman's Z-score model. *SSRN Electronic Journal*.

Spiegler, R. (2014). Competitive framing. *American Economic Journal: Microeconomics*, *6*(3), 35–58.

Sulaiman, E. K. (n.d.). *An empirical analysis of financial risk tolerance and demographic features of individual investors*. PsycEXTRA dataset. doi:https://doi.org/10.1037/e582862013-004.

Taillard, M. (2013). *Corporate finance for dummies*. Hoboken, NJ: John Wiley & Sons.

Taillard, M. (2015). *Personal finance: A practical guide*. London: Icon Books.

Taillard, M. (2016). *Economics and modern warfare: The invisible fist of the market*. Palgrave Macmillan.

Taillard, M. (2017a). *Aspirational revolution: The purpose-driven economy*. S.l.: Palgrave Macmillan.

Taillard, M. (2017b). *Cultural influences of investing behavior: A correlational design study*. ProQuest Dissertations Publishing.

Taillard, M., & Giscoppa, H. (2013). *Psychology and modern warfare: Idea management in conflict and competition*. New York, NY: Palgrave Macmillan.

Tversky, A., & Kahneman, D. (1973). *Availability: A heuristic for judging frequency and probability*. New York: Academic Press.

Tversky, A., & Kahneman, D. (1990). *Reference theory of choice and exchange*. Stanford, CA: Stanford Center on Conflict and Negotiation, Stanford University.

Tversky, A., Griffin, D., Heath, C., & Slovic, P. (1990). *Decision under conflict: Resolution and confidence in judgment and choice*. Stanford, CA: Dept. of Psychology, Stanford University.

Wong, S. (1978). *Foundations of Paul Samuelson's revealed preference theory: A study by the method of rational reconstruction*. Routledge.

World Investment Report (2015). Global value chains: Investment and trade for development. In *United Nations conference on trade and development (2013)* (pp. 1–264). Print.

Wu, L., & Brynjolfsson, E. (2012). The future of prediction: How Google searches foreshadow housing prices and sales. *SSRN Electronic Journal*. http://dx.doi.org/10.2139/ssrn.2022293.

Xu, Y., Hu, S., & Fan, X. (2009). The impacts of country risk and cultural distance on transnational equity investments. *Chinese Management Studies*, *3*(3), 235–248.

Index

Printed in the United States
By Bookmasters